Scenarios for Singles

Sketches and Scriptures Signifying a Master Plan

Annette Richardson

iUniverse, Inc.
Bloomington

Scenarios for Singles
Sketches and Scriptures Signifying a Master Plan

iUniverse books may be ordered through booksellers or by contacting:

iUniverse
1663 Liberty Drive
Bloomington, IN 47403
www.iuniverse.com
1-800-Authors (1-800-288-4677)

Because of the dynamic nature of the Internet, any web addresses or links contained in this book may have changed since publication and may no longer be valid. The views expressed in this work are solely those of the author and do not necessarily reflect the views of the publisher, and the publisher hereby disclaims any responsibility for them.

Any people depicted in stock imagery provided by Thinkstock are models, and such images are being used for illustrative purposes only.

Certain stock imagery © Thinkstock.

ISBN: 978-1-4759-1720-8 (sc)
ISBN: 978-1-4759-1721-5 (hc)
ISBN: 978-1-4759-1722-2 (e)

Printed in the United States of America

iUniverse rev. date: 5/24/2012

This book is lovingly dedicated to my Lord and Savior, Jesus Christ. Thank You, Lord, for making all things possible.

"Let the word of Christ dwell in you richly as you teach and admonish one another with all wisdom…. And whatever you do, whether in word or deed, do it all in the name of the Lord Jesus giving thanks to God the Father through him" (Colossians 3:16–17).

Contents

Preface

Scenarios for Singles is a compilation of twenty-six scenarios that portray Christian singles facing a range of personal dilemmas. Each scenario or case has a four-fold lesson plan that includes a case study, a sketch, group interaction and Bible study. Through these tools, your study group will seek to find viable solutions for the case study subjects in a single session.

As a psych major, I initially wanted to write a book that analyzed the complexities of making good choices versus bad choices, which would have been the perfect lead-in for Larry Kohlberg's theory of moral development. I would have then built onto Kohlberg's theory by adding the steps of obtaining self-actualization based on Maslow's hierarchy of needs. From Maslow, I would have moved on to Sir Francis Galton's great debate involving nature versus nurture. Once Sir Galton was presented, there is no way I could have omitted Freud's theory of personality. I have always had a burning desire to clarify that the *id* is really what laymen call the *ego* and the *superego* is really where our morals reside and so on and so forth.

I wanted to give everyone a brief psych 101 refresher with diagrams, charts, and graphs. From there, I would have moved on to the Bible. Yet, through His holy and gentle Spirit, the Lord led me another way. I sensed He was guiding me to keep the book simple, and that is what I've done. The bottom line is that God has already shown us through His wonderful Word how to make wiser decisions. He has shown us how to seek His will. No psychological theory can match a solid relationship with the true Logos. When we choose to ignore or disobey His Word, we continue to make bad choices. Sadly, bad choices lead to sin. It's as simple as that; no diagrams needed.

I am aware that the intricacies of sin are not always simple or straightforward. I do not pretend to have cut-and-dried answers to each scenario depicted in this book. I do believe, however, that studying and obeying the Word of God, along with diligent prayer, should always be the chief resources of Christian guidance and instruction.

Displayed in many of the cases throughout the book are examples of Christian singles who have not used all of these resources. Some of the sketches are deliberately oversimplified, with no complexities whatsoever in the resolution process. Some, on the other hand, are a little tougher to figure out. My objective was not to solve every given situation with pat answers or generic clichés. Rather, it was to help people within your group to start talking and thinking about the way Christian singles are making decisions. How are singles impacting the lives of others with the challenges they face? With what decision-making tools and skills are they equipped? From what sources are they drawing their conclusions? Are they drawing from the riches of God's Word or even from the wisdom of a godly pastor? You may find the answer to be discouraging.

A vast number of decisions made by Christian singles have no basis in the Word of God whatsoever. Regrettably, many Christians take the world's view instead of the Word's view on many of life's decisions due to ignorance. Let's face it: some topics are simply not discussed in a traditional church setting. Therefore, many Christian singles are not properly equipped to make godly choices. They are unable to defend their faith, make wise relationship choices, budget money, or handle a host of other situations. They're simply not being taught how. Most church and evangelistic programs are geared strictly toward a nuclear family life, but the reality of the nuclear family no longer fits everyone.

The harvest of singles is plentiful. What a glorious opportunity for church laborers. If singles are strengthened in Christ then marriages, families, churches, and societies will be strengthened. Today's Christian singles are complex, multifaceted souls in need—period. Yet they are often overlooked, ignored, judged, or just plain forgotten within the body of Christ. Of course, this is not the case in every church, but is it the case in your church?

Acknowledgements

I would like to express my gratitude to my immediate family members; my mother Leola, and to my sisters Dorothea, and Carlotta. I would also like to express my appreciation to my sisters and brothers in Christ who encouraged me to write this book. They are: Karen, Velisha, Susan, Sabrina, Kim, Lori, Jackie, Diane, Paulette, Carolyn, Cora, Edward, Dewayne, James and Charles; to my aunts Helen, Doris, Mildred and Lorine; to my extended family, my church family (especially those in Brother Wood's Sunday school class) and to my beloved friends. Thank you for your prayers, you support, and your diligence in helping to make this book become a reality.

Ways to Use This Book

Following are some tips that will make this book more helpful for readers:

- Welcome Jesus to your group with open arms, and ask Him for His guidance within the ministry.
- Pray *for* and *with* the members of your singles group before each session.
- If possible, try to use a different set of participants in your group to act out the roles during each study session.
- The facilitator may read the entire scenario aloud or may appoint someone else to do so.
- Make sure that the roles are actually performed in each session and not simply read aloud.
- No acting directions were added on purpose. Please don't hesitate to ad lib.
- Revamp the characters as needed.
- Be flexible. It may be necessary to enhance or reduce the direction of the lesson to fit the size of your group.
- Before each performance, the facilitator may shout, "*Role* it!" (not *roll* it) and "action!" This command acts as a cue to the performers to assume their respective roles. It's also fun to do.
- Discuss the characters and their motives and behaviors.
- Please note that some of the case studies presented are extremely controversial in content. Pray for God's peace to rest on each participant.

- Please keep personal information that is shared within the group.
- Read the scriptures *aloud* in your group.
- Really get to know the people in your group.
- Love God; love each other.
- Pray for and with the members of your group after each session.
- Hug someone next to you.
- Smile.

Session 1

Doug and Danielle—
Coming Clean

Doug and Danielle were Christians who had been engaged for nearly two years. They attended the same Christian university and happened to meet during a Christmas party at a mutual friend's house. When they met, they hit it off immediately and were engaged within six months.

As a couple, their relationship had a solid foundation. They both shared similar outlooks on life and had good family backgrounds. They also had sound work ethics and strong ties to the church. Together they had worked hard to save money toward their projected wedding expenses and a good down payment on their dream house.

Initially, Doug was very sure of his feelings toward Danielle. She was smart, kindhearted, warm, and very loving. She was the woman he wanted as his wife and the mother of his children. He had never doubted his love for Danielle until he met her younger sister, Dana.

Doug and Dana met during Thanksgiving dinner at his future in-laws' house. When his eyes met hers, the force of his attraction literally took his breath away. Dana was stunningly beautiful. For nearly eight months afterward, he prayed and struggled with his feelings toward Dana, but they had not gone away. He didn't understand what was happening to him. He had only seen Dana four times in his life! He knew he genuinely loved Danielle, but he could not ignore his attraction for Dana any longer.

FACILITATOR:	Role it and action!
DOUG:	Danielle, there is something I've wanted to say to you for quite some time, but I haven't known where to start.
DANIELLE:	Oh, Doug, I hope it's not bad news. The only thing that kept me going today was the thought of us having a nice, quiet dinner together.
DOUG:	Really?
DANIELLE:	Sweetheart, I love you so much! The idea of us being married and having our own place together is the light at the end of the tunnel for me. I love the fact that we're working together to build our future and that you're always there for me.
DOUG:	Danielle, I wish I could always be here for you, but what I have to tell you isn't going to be good news. In fact, it's going to be painful.
DANIELLE:	Painful? Doug, what's wrong? You're not sick, are you?
DOUG:	Physically, I feel fine, Danielle, but I guess there's no other way to tell you this except for me to get right to the point. I'm sorry if this hurts you, but I've had feelings for your sister Dana since I met her at your parents' house last Thanksgiving. The truth is that I think I'm in love with her, and I can't marry you while I have such strong feelings for her.

What do we say? How might Danielle respond? (Allow Danielle's character to ad lib.) Was Doug right to go first to Danielle with his feelings, or should he have told Dana first? Was he right to share his feelings, or should he have kept quiet and waited for them to eventually go away? What's this couple's next step? Discuss.

What does the *Word* say? Read scriptures from: Deuteronomy 23:21–23; Numbers 30:2; Matthew 5:33–37; Proverbs 3:3–8, 12:22, 13:5, 20:6; Ecclesiastes 5:1–2, 4–6; Romans 12:9–10, 12:17–18; 1 Corinthians 10:12–13, 23–24; James 5:16; Colossians 4:6; Philippians 4:13; and 1 Peter 3:10–11.

Determine which scriptures apply to each person involved in this case. Can you think of any scriptures to add? In the notes section below, write down your preferred scripture regarding this situation. Memorize it.

Notes

_____

_____

_____

_____

_____

_____

_____

_____

_____

_____

_____

Session 2

When Rebels Engage

Cheryl divorced her ex-husband Larry, exactly eight months, four days and thirteen hours ago. Her parents were right about him, but at the time she didn't care. She was in love. So she ignored their warnings and married him. He was not a Christian but he was a good man; so she thought. Once he put the wedding band on her finger, she was quickly introduced to the *real* Larry. Like the devil parading himself as an angel of light, he had concealed his true nature before they were married.

She tried to be a good wife, but he never appreciated her. He beat her, demeaned her, and scorned her belief in Christ. He taunted and humiliated her mercilessly in front of their children and his wisecracking friends. She came to the point where she hated her life. If it were not for her daughters, she couldn't have found the strength to keep going. She finally left him. She could not tolerate his cruel and oppressive behavior any longer.

Then she met Garrett, a kind, well-educated man who returned to his hometown after being away for twenty years. He was the district manager of a chain of upscale men's clothing stores and had recently joined the church where Cheryl held her membership. She liked what she saw and quickly insinuated herself into his life. She loved his flair. From his expensively cut suits to his luxury car, everything about him exuded success.

They could talk for hours on any subject. His ideas were innovative and unconventional. She found his live-and-let-live attitude very liberating. Compared to the extensive arguments she engaged in with Larry, Garrett's words were like splashes of cool, refreshing water in the heat of a mid-summer's day.

Six months later, when Garrett asked Cheryl to marry him and then presented her with an eye-popping, to-die-for, princess-cut diamond ring, she eagerly accepted his proposal. As Garrett's fiancée, she felt whole again. It moved her to tears. She was able to hold her head up high among her family and friends once more. She constantly dismissed the minor things she noticed about Garrett's demeanor that made her uneasy at times and refused to dwell on anything that didn't enhance her overall happiness.

She continued to suppress her niggling doubts until she ran into Tara, her old high school rival. During their conversation, Tara gave her some very disturbing information. Initially Cheryl disregarded it, putting it down as petty gossip and jealousy. However, as she looked back, she remembered being surprised to learn that Garrett had never married. At the time, he told her that he'd always wanted a family of his own. He simply hadn't met the right person until he met her. After that, she hadn't mentioned it again. She also noticed that there was only a slight difference in the way he treated her and the way he treated her daughters. Since he was twelve years her senior, she assumed *that* was the sole reason for his avuncular affection toward her.

She had to talk to Garrett about it. Cheryl prayed for the first time since her divorce. She told God that if He gave her another chance, she would no longer remain angry with Him about Larry and she would make her second marriage work by any means necessary.

FACILITATOR:	Role it and action!
GARRETT:	That was an excellent dinner, Cheryl. You certainly outdid yourself. Why don't you let me do the dishes before we sit down to watch the movie you rented?
CHERYL:	That's sweet of you, thanks.
GARRETT:	What's the matter, honey? You seem a little preoccupied tonight. Did you have a bad day?
CHERYL:	Garrett, could you hold off for a minute with the dishes? I heard something rather disturbing the other day when I was at the mall, and I wanted to talk to you about it.
GARRETT:	Disturbing? What did you hear, and why did you find it disturbing?

CHERYL:	Before I get into all of that, do you know a woman named Tara Hodges? She went to Roosevelt High. She's an old classmate of mine.
GARRETT:	Hmm … Hodges. No, I don't think so. Did she say she knew me?
CHERYL:	No, not exactly.
GARRETT:	Well, dear, what exactly did she say?
CHERYL:	She said that when her older brother Tim went away to college, he came out of the closet and had a sexual affair with a guy they called Gee. She said that the two were quite an item on campus. They rebelled against the campus regulations and openly lived as a gay couple. I know that you went to the same college Tim did, so I started to wonder.
GARRETT:	You started to wonder what? If I knew this guy named Gee?
CHERYL:	Yes … well, I mean no. I mean—oh, I don't know what I mean! I'm sorry, it's just the things she said upset me so badly. They were confusing to me, and I don't know what to think. Oh, Garrett!
GARRETT:	Go ahead, Cheryl, and say what's on your mind.
CHERYL:	All right, Garrett, when she described this Gee person, she gave an exact description of you—I mean right down to the tattoo on your right arm. *Are* you and Gee the same guy?
GARRETT:	Cheryl dear, the truth is that none of us are who we were twenty years ago. We need to let bygones be bygones. You know, live and let live? The only thing that's important now is that you trust me. I love you and the girls, and you love me. That's all that matters, isn't it?

What do we say? How should Cheryl respond? Did Garrett answer her question in a satisfying way? Should engaged couples thoroughly discuss their past relationships? Is it better not to know? Was Cheryl's prayer more of a monologue than a dialogue? How are Cheryl and Garrett rebels? Discuss.

What does the *Word* say? Read scriptures from: Proverbs 19:3, 28:13, 17:11, 8:13; Leviticus 18:22; Matthew 7:1–2; Ephesians 4:26–27, 5:11–14; 1 Corinthians 7:13, 6:9–11, 18–20; 2 Corinthians 5:17–18; Romans 1:24–28, 3:23, 14:12–13; and James 1:19–21.

Determine which scriptures apply to each person involved in this case. Can you think of any scriptures to add? In the notes section below, write down your preferred scripture regarding this situation. Memorize it.

Notes

_____

_____

_____

_____

_____

_____

_____

_____

_____

_____

_____

Session 3

Session 3

Terri and Kenneth—the Pursuit of Happiness

Terri was single, an active Sunday school teacher and seeing a married man. The relationship started out strictly as a friendship. It began mostly because she felt sorry for Kenneth and his son, Alex. There were times when Kenneth and his son would stay at the church long after everyone else had gone home. Kenneth would often stay and help Terri clean up after children's church activities while Alex huddled in a corner doing homework or sleeping. She knew in her heart that something was wrong, but she didn't want to pry.

One Friday evening after a large cleanup from Vacation Bible School activities, Kenneth came up to Terri. He offered to buy her dinner to celebrate the end of VBS. Alex had gone to spend the weekend at a friend's house, and Kenneth said he would appreciate her company. She accepted. Terri's heart was touched by his obvious need for companionship.

During the course of the meal, Kenneth told Terri many things that had gone wrong in his marriage. He told her that he had been with his wife, Andrea, for ten agonizing years. He begged Terri to understand how he desperately wanted out of his hell of a marriage. He admitted that Alex was the only good thing that had come from the marriage. He then broke down and cried when he disclosed the pain of a miscarriage Andrea had experienced after Alex was born. Terri's heart broke for him, and she cried too.

After the miscarriage, the marriage and Andrea's mental health rapidly deteriorated. Doctors had strongly advised counseling and treatment for her postpartum depression. Andrea had refused counseling, and their house became a war zone. Each one blamed the other for all the things that had gone wrong in the marriage. Andrea believed Kenneth was trying to turn Alex away from her. She said Kenneth had abandoned her emotionally and spiritually, and she suspected he was having an affair. Physical intimacy was the last thing on earth she wanted from him. When Kenneth said those words, Terri's heart ached for him.

Kenneth confessed that he too thought counseling was a waste of time. Their marriage was over. He wondered how any doctor though he could cure the rantings of a madwoman such as Andrea. He had witnessed that when Andrea couldn't get her way, she screamed and howled like a banshee. He thought she should be locked up. The police had been called to their house several times, but they never arrested her. He believed she only behaved that way to get attention. It was her way of trying to control him. Terri's heart went out to him.

He also knew that control was the real reason she abstained from having sex with him. She did it to punish him because he had been away on business when she lost their baby. It was all a control game that selfish women had played for centuries to torment their husbands. Therefore, he had come up with a plan of his own. To avoid all of the crying and emotional drama at home, he had rented a hotel room for him and Alex. Kenneth went to work, dropped his son off at school, and picked him up. From there they grabbed some food and then headed for church. That was his life. Terri's heart longed for him.

Then Kenneth shared how truly grateful he and Alex were for Terri's kindness. He wanted her to know how much he enjoyed working with her in the church's youth ministry. He believed it brought them closer together and also closer to the Lord. He was sure that God had sent His comfort through her. She made Kenneth happy and had been a much-needed bright spot in his otherwise dreary life. Terri's heart filled with love for him.

FACILITATOR:	Role it and action!
KENNETH:	Terri, I am so in love with you. I really believe that the Lord has put you in my life as a special gift to me because He knew my marriage was suffering. We have so much in common. You love the church as much as I do, and you are devoted to the youth ministry, which is precious

in God's sight. I just know you and I are meant
to be together. You're everything I've ever
wanted.

TERRI: I love you too, Kenny, but I don't know where
to go from here.

KENNETH: I know that's troubling you. You don't want to
continue seeing me because I'm still married.
Well, the truth is, I plan to ask Andrea for a
divorce this weekend. I can't go on this way.
She and I have been so miserable, and it's time
to cut our losses. I know the Lord does not
want me to stay trapped in a hopeless, unhappy
marriage. He doesn't want me to be with a
woman who will no longer have sex and who
doesn't know how to make a man feel like a
man. He doesn't want me with a woman who
doesn't love me.

TERRI: Oh, Kenny, I know she's mistreated you terribly,
but what about Alex? Would he want to live
with us? Once the divorce is final, would he stay
with us or with his mother?

KENNETH: You would be his mother. I think the courts
will grant me custody if they knew the kind of
psycho she's been. When this is all over, we can
truly be a real family—a happy family.

TERRI: Kenny, I don't believe that all of your suffering
has been in vain. This must be God's will for
each of us and for our lives together. He wants
us to be happy. We can't lose our chance at true
happiness.

What do we say? As a Christian, unmarried woman, how should Terri
conduct herself around Kenneth? Should an unmarried person go out to
dinner with a married person; one of the opposite sex who is not a relative?
Why? If she loves Kenneth, shouldn't she be there for him? Is Kenneth
right? Does God want him to be free from an unhappy marriage? What
kind of example is Kenneth setting for Alex? Discuss.

What does the *Word* say? Read scriptures from: Malachi 2:13–16;
James 1:13–15; Ephesians 5:3, 5:25; Phillipians 2:21; James 4:7; Hebrews

13:4; 1 Corinthians 13:4–7, 6:9–11, 15:33–34; Matthew 19:9, 5:28, 18:6; Isaiah 5:20; and Colossians 3:5.

Determine which scriptures apply to each person involved in this case. Can you think of any scriptures to add? In the notes section below, write down your preferred scripture regarding this situation. Memorize it.

Notes

_____
_____
_____
_____
_____
_____
_____
_____
_____
_____
_____

Session 4

Derrick and Tiffany— Made for Each Other

Derrick and Tiffany are the new *it* couple within their circle of friends and associates. They first met at the city's civic center during the Professional Women's charity luncheon. The event was held annually for top businesswomen and their families. Derrick had come dutifully to the luncheon at his mother Gertrude's command, and so had his father, Edward. According to Gertrude, it was high time Derrick was married. She informed her husband that she would take matters into her own hands and find their son the right kind of wife. The Professional Women's luncheon would be an ideal place to find prospective brides. The young women who attended were from affluent families, with good breeding and bright futures. Edward said nothing.

Under his mother's watchful eye, Derrick sat next to Tiffany. Gertrude's approval became more apparent as the couple's conversation and attraction grew. Derrick and Tiffany were total opposites of each other but quite smitten.

From their first encounter, Derrick was immediately aware that he and Tiffany were like day and night. She was a fast talker. He was not. She had tons of friends. He had a few. She was pretty and fun-loving. He often felt old and stuffy. Her greatest attribute was her extreme wealth whereas he was only middle class. She was also spontaneous, and when she asked him on a date, he couldn't say no. He usually liked to make the first move toward the opposite sex, but he found Tiffany's boldness and self-assurance exciting. Gertrude was delighted with Derrick's decision to go out with Tiffany, but his father was not.

After they had dated for several months, Tiffany was not as delighted with Derrick the fiancé as she had been with Derrick the new boyfriend; however, she had gotten used to his ways, and she wanted to be married. Nearly all of her friends were wives and mothers. Derrick would fit in perfectly with her plans. He was good-looking and malleable, which made him good husband material. She knew he was uptight about money. She tolerated his views on religion and politics, and his ideas on sex were a little tedious, but she would bring him around. She was determined. After all, she had gotten him to propose.

With Derrick's ring on her finger, she persuaded her father to send top clients his way. Derrick's reputation in the community began to grow, and so did his business, due to her father's connections. He owed Tiffany and she planned to collect from him big time. She wasn't worried that he'd been slow to agree on a wedding date. She had money, her father's connections and Gertrude on her side. Together they would make the marriage happen.

She did have *some* concern though about Derrick's father. She couldn't even coax a smile from the dried-up little man. She was convinced that he didn't like her and God only knew why not. She had bent over backward for the little prune but she hadn't gotten anything from him. She and Derrick would marry before the end of summer; by then, Edward could either like it or lump it. She had already made most of the arrangements for the wedding. Derrick *would* be her husband and the father of her children. She wouldn't take no for an answer. She would get him down the aisle by any means necessary.

FACILITATOR:	Role it and action!
TIFFANY:	Derrick, why are you frowning, again? Honestly, darling, you frown too much these days. I told you Daddy would pay for the new car.
DERRICK:	I know you did, but I'm you fiancée. You should have asked me first, not your father.
TIFFANY:	I didn't want to hear a lecture, so I went to Daddy.
DERRICK:	The car you're driving now is not even a year old. Darling, you just don't *need* another new car.

TIFFANY: I know, but I *want* a new car. I want the new one to show off at my bridal shower, and I need the other one for my bachelorette party.

DERRICK: I hope you know that after we're married, all this impulse spending will have to stop.

TIFFANY: Why are you so upset? The car is as much for you as it is for me. Daddy will pay for anything we want. Look at it as one of our many, many wedding gifts.

DERRICK: That's not the point, darling. Once we get married, I don't want you to go running to your father every time you want something. We'll need to get you on a budget. The spoiled brat routine will have to end. Do you understand?

TIFFANY: I'm not a brat! I simply believe there's no sense in having money if you can't enjoy spending it.

DERRICK: If you must know, that's the very reason why I can't decide on a date for us to marry—because we can't see eye to eye on your spending!

TIFFANY: You can't be serious. If I want something and *you* can't afford it, I'm going to ask Daddy for it. As a matter of fact, you can count on it. As for a wedding date, June 12 will be perfect at St. Paul's. I've already booked it. It's the church where I was baptized, and it's the perfect backdrop for our wedding. If you don't think June 12 is a good time, I think I'll have to tell Daddy that I'm pregnant.

DERRICK: That's a lie, and you know it! It's also blackmail! Would you stoop to lying to your own father to get your way?

TIFFANY: In a New York minute. So what do you say, June 12 at St. Paul's? Don't you think you owe me that much, darling?

What do we say? Do opposites attract? How should Derrick answer Tiffany? Does Tiffany have the right attitude about money? Why would Gertrude and Tiffany get along so well together? What's with Edward? Why would he dislike Tiffany? Discuss.

What does the *Word* say? Read scriptures from: Matthew 6:19–21, 24, 16:26; 1 Timothy 6:9–10; Proverbs 3:5–6, 16:19, 19:14, 21:2, 19; Ecclesiastes 5:10; Philippians 2:3; Hebrews 13:5; and James 5:1–6.

Determine which scriptures apply to each person involved in this case. Can you think of any scriptures to add? In the notes section below, write down your preferred scripture regarding this situation. Memorize it.

Notes

_____

_____

_____

_____

_____

_____

_____

_____

_____

_____

Session 5

Marvin and Maria—the Complexion of Love

Melvin is an African American male and Maria is a Latina. They were both very active in campus multicultural and diversity student organizations. They met when Melvin needed a tutor to help him pass his second-year Spanish course and Maria needed a tutor for a chemistry class. They were assigned to each other as tutors through the multicultural affairs office. During their tutoring sessions, they discussed a variety of things and found that they were very sympathetic to the plight of minorities in America. Being empathetic to the other's hurts, they soon found that even though they were both from different backgrounds, they had more in common than they had differences. Melvin and Maria worked very hard to help each other pass their respective courses.

When their exams were over, they went out to dinner to celebrate. They had been together for two years as a couple after that first dinner date when friendship grew into love and Melvin asked Maria to marry him. She agreed. Though they had spoken many times of family and religious traditions, neither of them had deep ties to any particular church—or so they thought.

FACILITATOR:	Role it and action!
MELVIN:	Have you told your family yet?

MARIA:	You mean have I told them that we're planning to get married after we graduate, or have I told them that you're black?
MELVIN:	Both.
MARIA:	I told my parents that you are black, and they did not have a problem with it.
MELVIN:	So why do you still have a worried look on your face?
MARIA:	Well, it's not that you're black that's the problem.
MELVIN:	I'm glad to hear that being black isn't a problem. So what *is* the problem?
MARIA:	I told them that I love you, that you treat me very well, that you're studying to become a dentist, and that you are a good Christian man.
MELVIN:	That all sounds good, Maria. Now what's the problem?
MARIA:	My parents are devout Catholics, Melvin, and when we marry, they want us to be married in the cathedral by our priest.
MELVIN:	I don't attend church much these days, but I never saw our beliefs as being problematic. I thought you believed in the same Jesus I do.
MARIA:	I do believe in Jesus, and since it's the same Jesus, I don't think it's a big deal, do you?
MELVIN:	No, I don't. My parents are dyed-in-the-wool Baptists, but I'm sure they wouldn't have any problem with your beliefs.
MARIA:	Have you told your parents that I'm a Latina and Catholic?
MELVIN:	No, I haven't.
MARIA:	What are you waiting for, Melvin? Are you afraid there will be a fight?"
MELVIN:	I'm not afraid, but I am tired of the fighting. Listen, my folks are good people.
MARIA:	Okay, your folks are good people, but what?
MELVIN:	But my sister, Kenya, just recently married a guy named Amir.
MARIA:	So? What does that have to do with us?

MELVIN:	It has nothing to do with us directly. The thing is, Amir is Muslim, and last Christmas at my parents' house was not very merry. In fact, it was like a war zone. The whole Allah being the same as the Christian God, Yahweh, was a bad holiday topic. It really didn't go well with the eggnog.
MARIA:	Wow, as much as we've talked about religion, Melvin, you've never told me about your sister and Amir.
MELVIN:	I didn't want to scare you off.
MARIA:	I'm not scared. I just want to know if there's anything else you're keeping from me.
MELVIN:	Well, to tell you the truth, my mother is going to flip when she finds out you're not African American.
MARIA:	Seriously? Are you're saying that your mom may accept that I'm Catholic but she won't accept that I'm a Latina?
MELVIN:	She'll come around in time, babe.
MARIA:	Oh, Melvin!
MELVIN:	I love you. C'mon, say it with me.

What do we say? What are some things Melvin and Maria should do before meeting either set of parents or agreeing to marry? What are the major differences and similarities in what Catholics and Baptists believe? What are the major differences and similarities in what Christians and Muslims believe? Besides religion, what are some other problems Melvin and Maria may face as a couple? Discuss.

What does the *Word* say? Read scriptures from: James 1:2–5, 26–27; Psalm 111:10; Colossians 3:11; Numbers 12:1–15; 2 Corinthians 6:14; John 7:24, 13:34; 1 John 2:9; Acts 10:34–35; Matthew 10:34–36; 1 Peter 3:13–15; and Colossians 2:8.

Determine which scriptures apply to each person involved in this case. Can you think of any scriptures to add? In the notes section below, write down your preferred scripture regarding this situation. Memorize it.

Notes

_____

_____

_____

_____

_____

_____

_____

_____

_____

_____

_____

Session 6

Estelle and Stan—
Hooking Up over Sixty

Estelle is a sixty-nine-year-old widow. Her husband, Arthur, had already retired from the railroad when he died three years ago. After his death, she began to receive a monthly pension check that allowed her to live comfortably. Although she was doing well financially, she missed her husband and longed for someone special in her life. Both of her children lived in different states, and she often felt lonely. Then she met Stan. Stan was easy to talk to, fun, and a Christian man with Christian values.

Lately, Stan had talked seriously about marriage. Estelle cared for Stan deeply, but she was not sure if they could live on his income only. If they married, her widow's pension check would stop. Estelle frankly did not want to lose the security of her dead husband's provision, nor did she want to lose Stan. She wanted him in her life indefinitely, but how could she afford to have him?

FACILITATOR:	Role it and action!
STAN:	Estelle, you know that after Sylvia died, I didn't date for years until I met you. When I met you, I wanted to be in a relationship again.
ESTELLE:	Stan, I think I know where this conversation is going and I don't think—
STAN:	Hold on now and listen. We've been seeing each other for more than a year, and I would like for

	you to think about us getting married. Neither of us is getting any younger, you know.
ESTELLE:	Stan, I do really care about you. You've been a godsend to me but—
STAN:	Well, then what's the problem? I love you. Don't you love me?
ESTELLE:	Yes, of course I do, but wouldn't it be more practical if we lived together? Don't you think it's smarter than marrying? We're old enough to know our own minds. Besides, who would care?
STAN:	Did you say live together? Why, Estelle, we're both Christians. We can't just up and live together before God as husband and wife without being married.
ESTELLE:	If I marry you, I won't receive my widow's pension from Arthur. The government will also cut the amount of our Social Security checks.
STAN:	We'll make it, baby, don't worry.
ESTELLE:	Both of our spouses died rather suddenly, which kept hospital expenses down a little except for funeral costs, but what if one of us gets really sick? Let's face it, Stan; you're not a rich man. The extra money from Arthur would come in handy. We could always use the extra money.

What do we say? What does Stan need to establish with Estelle? Is Estelle correct in saying that nobody minds moral obligations once you get older? Discuss.

What does the *Word* say? Read scriptures from: Hebrews 13:4, 1 Corinthians 6:10, 18–20; Proverbs 3:5, 16:31; Isaiah 54:4–5; Jeremiah 29:11; 1 John 4:18; Romans 12:1–2; Psalm 71:9, 37:25; Matthew 6:25–34; Titus 2:2–3; and Philippians 4:6–7.

Determine which scriptures apply to each person involved in this case. Can you think of any scriptures to add? In the notes section below, write down your preferred scripture regarding this situation. Memorize it.

Notes

_____

_____

_____

_____

_____

_____

_____

_____

_____

_____

_____

Session 7

Angela's In-Crowd In-Laws

Since her divorce, Angela found it nearly impossible to attend church without experiencing some type of negative backlash from fellow church members. Her ex-husband, Mark, and his family were members of the same church as well. Through the years, Mark's family had made huge donations to the church, and they were large contributors to the church's building fund. Her ex-father-in-law, Tom, was a longtime trustee and had a great deal of influence in church politics. He had deep connections with city officials and was said to be made of Teflon. Mark was his father's right-hand man. Tom's wife, Edna, was also a chief decision maker in both municipal and church planning. If her husband was made of Teflon, then Edna was made of iron. Before the divorce, Angela had been Edna's right hand and noted protégée.

Edna presided over an elite group of women who were made up of deacons, trustees, and associate ministers' wives. They were the church's movers and shakers. These handful of women determined whether a church activity or auxiliary was deemed valid or invalid. They decided *who* and *what* was important in church ministry.

As Mark's wife, Angela had been asked to chair several statewide women's conferences, banquets, committees, and seminars. Her influence had numerous church auxiliary members and guilds vying for her leadership. The offers to sit on community boards had been abundant. With Mark's influence and connections, they were invited to dinners and social events nearly every weekend.

Since the divorce, however, all social phone calls, e-mails, and invitations had ceased. Little by little, she had been excluded from her old circle of friends. As her children looked on in confusion, Angela had experienced social avoidance, a distinct lack of eye contact, tight smiles, and the cold shoulder treatment. All of it had really taken its toll. She felt as though she had lost her citizenship, and she saw no way of returning to the elite status.

Lately, hushed whispers and marked silences when she entered a room made her feel awful. Her one true friend, Mrs. Ames, was the only one who had not abandoned her. She discreetly let Angela know that her mother-in-law, Edna, had spread a number of spiteful rumors at the last ushers' meeting. Mrs. Ames assured her that these things would pass. Angela was not sure she could hold on while the church members continued to shun her.

Angela tried to speak to her pastor, but he seemed reluctant to talk to her for more than five minutes. She didn't want to leave the church and uproot her children, but the alienation was becoming unbearable. She didn't know how long she could continue to be treated like a leper.

FACILITATOR:	Role it and action!
ANGELA:	Mrs. Ames, I don't know what to do about staying on at church.
MRS. AMES:	Why, Angie? What have they done now?
ANGELA:	Well, Kelly came home crying after church on Sunday. She said that one of the children called her an ugly name.
MRS. AMES:	I'm so sorry, dear.
ANGELA:	So am I. Sometimes I feel like I can't stay at that church for another second, and to think I used to be among the very people who have turned their backs on me now. It hurts so badly. I just don't think I can stay any longer.
MRS. AMES:	If you leave, Angela, where would you go? Your in-laws are very influential people.
ANGELA:	I know, but I can't continue to have my children exposed to taunts and lies.
MRS. AMES:	Yes, and rumors started by their own grandmother. It's a shame.

ANGELA:	I know. Edna is really a good grandmother to the children, but Mark has filled her head with such lies about me. It was Mark who was unfaithful in the marriage.
MRS. AMES:	Have you considered going to her and telling her the truth about the things that happened in your marriage that led to the divorce?
ANGELA:	I'm not sure if she would believe me, but at this point, I honestly don't know what to do, Mrs. Ames.
MRS. AMES:	Grab my hand, dear, and let's pray. It's the best thing to do when you don't know what else to do.

What do we say? What are some options Angela has? What decision seems to be in the best interest of her children? Should she speak openly about her marriage to her mother-in-law? Should she speak to her ex-husband first? Discuss.

What does the *Word* say? Read scriptures from: Matthew 18:10–11, 15–17, 19:8–9, 7:12; Ephesians 4:29–31; 1 Timothy 5:1–2; Proverbs 15:4, 16:18–19; Psalm 145:14, 143:9–10; and Hebrews 10:25.

Determine which scriptures apply to each person involved in this case. Can you think of any scriptures to add? In the notes section below, write down your preferred scripture regarding this situation. Memorize it.

Notes

_____

_____

_____

_____

_____

_____

_____

_____

_____

_____

Session 8

David and the Giant Irony

David was a thirty-seven-year-old Christian man who loved the Lord and who also loved his freedom. David had absolutely no intention of ever marrying. He saw how divorce had destroyed his oldest brother, Cal, and he never wanted to go through that kind of agony over a woman. He was content with his birth family, his friends, and his work. He lived the life that most of his married buddies only dreamed of. He loved his job at Livewize Insured as a health insurance representative. Livewize allowed him the freedom to travel all over the world and to get paid for the journey. He found great fulfillment in his work. He believed God had given him the job to help families have affordable health care.

In his travels, he had met a number of women from all different walks of life. Although he professed Christ as his Savior, in moments of temptation, he had used women to satisfy his physical needs with very few regrets. His conscience gave him an occasional pang or two, but he would disregard the feelings of guilt. He never promised any of them any long-term commitments. Therefore, when it came time for each one to go their separate ways, no one had reason to complain. Any woman who entered into a relationship with him knew the score. He let them know that the relationship was strictly in the moment.

Daphne was his latest lady friend. She was beautiful, smart, and funny. Unfortunately, she had recently started to make noises about getting married. He reminded her that early on in their relationship, he had strictly told her there would be no marriage. David figured as long as she knew the facts up front, no harm, no foul. The choice was hers whether to stay in the relationship or to leave. No woman was smart enough to trap him into matrimony. So far he had been pretty successful in keeping his relationships with women right where he wanted, and Daphne would be no different.

Regrettably, he had not been as successful with his career as he had been in his personal life. He loved working for Livewize Insured, but it seemed that no matter how hard he tried, he could not get the recognition he deserved. His boss was a great guy. He always told David that he did exceptional work, but he had never offered David the position of AVP that he wanted the most. The one position that would move him further up the corporate ladder seemed totally out of reach. He worked hard, long hours and did all that he could think of to please his boss, but it was all in vain. In fact, David's boss had recently hired his coworker, Kate, for the position of assistant vice president.

FACILITATOR:	Role it and action!
DAVID:	Hey, Kate, I just wanted to say congratulations on the promotion to AVP in customer enhancement. Good job.
KATE:	Well, thank you, Dave. That certainly means a lot coming from you. Frankly, my biggest worry was that you would get the job, especially after that presentation you gave to the board last month.
DAVID:	Yeah, I thought I was a shoe-in. To be honest with you, I was furious when you got it and I didn't. Don't worry, though, I'm getting over it.
KATE:	I'm glad to hear it.
DAVID:	Yeah, but I can't understand what I keep doing wrong. I went back to school and got my degree in business. I took more insurance classes. I enrolled in leadership training courses. I took all the necessary requirements. I don't know what else to do.
KATE:	I really thought you would get the AVP position in sales two years ago, but it went to Sue. She *was* super qualified, though.

DAVID:	Sure, sure. The boss said it was a tough choice, but Sue had more experience in sales. I guess that's the reason.
KATE:	You shouldn't doubt yourself; I mean, it's obvious that he likes you. He always chooses you to go get the tough out-of town accounts, and you always deliver.
DAVID:	Yeah, I really shouldn't complain because the pay is great, but I can't seem to move beyond this position. I can't get promoted to AVP, and I know I'm qualified. AVP is the next step for me.
KATE:	What are you going to do now?
DAVID:	I've actually thought of leaving the company.
KATE:	Honestly? Would you really leave?
DAVID:	You know I've prayed about it, but I can't seem to get an answer. I don't want to leave. I've been here for fifteen years. I started off in the mail room and worked my way up. Right now, I just don't know what to do. I hope I have a shot for the AVP position in purchasing that's coming up when old John retires.
KATE:	I hate to say this, but rumor has it that Donna Perkins is the top runner for that position.
DAVID:	What? Are you serious?
KATE:	Hey, that's just what I've heard, but listen, now that you know what you're up against, you can make the choice whether to stay or leave, right? It's not like you don't know the facts up front.

What do we say? Name some reasons why David may not have received the recognition and the position he desires. Are there any similarities with his personal life and the things going on at his job? What kinds of things do you see? Does sin block us from success? How can David get on the right track with his work situation? How can he get on the right track with God? Discuss.

What does the *Word* say? Read scriptures from: Galatians 6:7–8; 1 Corinthians 6:18–20; Colossians 3:5; 1 John 3:6; Matthew 6:33, 5:16; Romans 3:23, 6:13; Psalm 51:10; Ephesians 5:3; 1 Thessalonians 4:2–8; and James 4:3, 7.

Determine which scriptures apply to each person involved in this case. Can you think of any scriptures to add? In the notes section below, write down your preferred scripture regarding this situation. Memorize it.

Notes

_____

_____

_____

_____

_____

_____

_____

_____

_____

_____

Session 9

Evelyn Reaps a Bitter Harvest

Evelyn was fed up with both of her children's behavior. They were totally out of control. Kevin was a grown man now and wouldn't listen to reason and Catlin's attitude had gotten progressively worse since her father, Joe, walked out on them. Joe had been a frustrated guitar player in a local band of burnouts who, in between gigs, raised hell, smoked pot, and drank heavily. Before he left, Joe generally stayed home during the day and watched Catlin while Evelyn went to wait tables to pay their rent. Evelyn and Joe had partied hard together, dropped some acid here and there, and they even dabbled occasionally in the occult. Evelyn had gotten involved with Joe and had been too afraid of him to get out of the relationship. Catlin was the product of their union.

Evelyn had never married Joe, nor was he Kevin's biological father. Kevin despised Joe because he was a mean drunk and would often beat him. Evelyn would try to stop Joe from beating Kevin, but he would then turn and beat her too. Needless to say, she had not been sorry to see him leave. When Joe left for good, Evelyn went back to her roots. Her parents had brought her up to pray and go to church, and she began to do those things again. She wanted to get her life back on track with the Lord.

Kevin had started to go to church with her and took on a part-time job after school to help with the bills. Eventually he stopped going to church and started working longer hours. Then he began to come home with more money. Sometimes he would have large wads of cash. Rena, his girlfriend who was ten years his senior, starting bringing people to their home. People would knock on Evelyn's door at all times of the day and night asking for Kevin.

Evelyn knew her son was selling drugs. She asked him to stop, but he said he was not selling. She kept quiet and pretended to believe him when he told her he'd earned extra money by working nights and weekends at his regular job. Evelyn tried to convince herself that they desperately needed the money, but after going back to church and hearing God's Word, she knew she had to stop rationalizing and pretending; yet she was afraid to confront Kevin.

To help her out, he took on more responsibilities as a big brother to Catlin when she got into trouble at school. She was eventually placed in counseling for self-mutilation and was diagnosed with bipolar disorder. It was Kevin who broke into the bathroom on Valentine's Day and found his sister on the bathroom floor, covered in blood from slashing her wrists. Later she admitted her boyfriend had dumped her. After that episode, Evelyn barely recognized Catlin.

As if dealing with her *daughter's* emotional problems wasn't enough, Kevin started to behave strangely. His disposition became secretive and moody. He came in one day after school and informed her that he was going to drop out of high school and receive his GED in another state. Prior to this bombshell, his odd behavior always seemed to coincide with watching the evening news. He finally announced to her that he planned to stay at Rena's house until the school year ended.

FACILITATOR:	Role it and action!
DOTTIE:	Evelyn, honey, how do you do it? I've been waitressing only for a few weeks, and my feet are killing me!
EVELYN:	Waitressing is a breeze, Dottie. It's being a good mother that's killing me.
DOTTIE:	Yeah, I was sorry to hear that Kevin got arrested on a drug deal that had been set up by the police. It was all over the news. I think it took a lot of courage for you to tell the police the truth.
EVELYN:	They gave him a lighter sentence since he's a minor, but Rena and her friends will do some hard time. He says he hates me and that I'm a traitor. He doesn't understand that cooperating

	with the police was the only way that I could keep him alive.
DOTTIE:	I'm sorry, Evelyn. So, what about Catlin? How is she holding up?
CATLIN:	She hates me too and threatens to run away from home every other day.
DOTTIE:	Do you think she will?
EVELYN:	I don't know, but I keep telling Catlin that someday she's going to reap what she sows. All she has to do is look at my life and see that I'm telling her the truth, but she won't listen. She's hardheaded. She gets angry and says she'll never be like me because all I do is read the Bible and nag. She told me once that my nagging is why Joe left. Then she said that I couldn't keep a man if I paid him top dollar.
DOTTIE:	Ouch! It's got to hurt to hear that kind of talk from your own flesh and blood.
EVELYN:	It's all right, Dottie. She'll learn. You should hear some of the things she says to me when she hasn't taken her meds. I can't believe she's the same little girl I used to rock to sleep.
EVELYN:	That's tough, Evelyn.
CATLIN:	Yeah, it's tough, but I'm holding on to my faith. I knew it wasn't going to be easy once I decided to get right with Jesus. I've sinned and made some big mistakes, and these are the consequences. I just hope I live to see my children come to know Christ as their Savior before I die. Maybe then they'll understand.

What do we say? Name some of the consequences of Evelyn's past behavior. Was she wrong to turn her son over to the authorities? Did her behavior exemplify love? How? Can dabbling in the occult affect a child's behavior? Do modern Christians believe in the existence of demons? What new steps can Evelyn take in disciplining her daughter? What are some ways to cultivate faith in the midst of trials?

What does the *Word* say? Read scriptures from: Galatians 5:19–21, 6:7; Numbers 14:18; Proverbs 10:1, 17:25, 19:18, 20:20, 29:15,17; Deuteronomy

5:16, 6:5–7, 18:10–13, 24:16; Ephesians 6:1–4, 12; 1 Samuel 15:22–23; Hebrews 12:11; Ecclesiastes 12:1; 1 Corinthians 13:11, 15:33–34; Leviticus 19:28; Ezekiel 18:20; Psalm 40:1; and Matthew 5:44–45, 10:34–39.

Determine which scriptures apply to each person involved in this case. Can you think of any scriptures to add? In the notes section below, write down your preferred scripture regarding this situation. Memorize it.

Notes

_____

_____

_____

_____

_____

_____

_____

_____

_____

_____

Session 10

Sam and Libby—That Was Then

Sam was a new Christian. He had a four-year-old son named Cody by his ex-girlfriend, Libby. When Sam became a Christian, he asked Libby to marry him, but she refused him twice. After months of trying to make things work with her, he moved out of their apartment and got his own place. Libby, in turn, latched on to Rick, her new boyfriend who helped her pay half the rent.

Sam and Libby shared responsibilities for Cody, but Sam did not like most of what his son was exposed to when he visited his mother. On his last visit, Cody had come back from Libby's apartment wearing nail polish, eyeliner, and pink hair bows. He also had been very hungry. He said he hadn't eaten anything except potato chips all that day. His clothes were dirty and smelled strongly of marijuana. It wasn't the first time he had come home hungry and smelling like pot.

Outraged, Sam called Libby and demanded to know what had been going on when he left Cody in her care. He let her know that she needed to feed Cody some decent food when he visited her. He also told her not to expose their son to drugs of any kind or let him wear anything made for girls. He told her if it continued, she would not see Cody again. Libby just laughed. She told him that Christianity had made him far too uptight and that he needed to relax. She assured him that there was plenty of food at her house but Cody didn't want what she had cooked. She then told him that all her friends thought Cody looked cute when he tapped into his feminine side. Sam was infuriated and could not find the humor in the situation, especially at his son's expense.

Before he came to know Christ as his Savior, Sam had many ideas that were contrary to the Word of God, but once he started to attend Bible study at his church and read the Word, the Holy Spirit began to show him the truth, and his heart was changed. He now wanted God's best for his son, but did that include Libby?

FACILITATOR:	Role it and action!
SAM:	Listen, Libby, since Jesus is now Lord and Savior of my life, I can't do the things I used to do in the past. That's why I'm telling you if you're getting high and letting Cody dress up like a girl, it has to stop. I don't want him around you when you're doing things like that.
LIBBY:	Dude, you are blowing things way out of proportion. You need to chill.
SAM:	Chill? Is that all you can say when my son came home smelling like pot and dressed up like Malibu Barbie? Chill?
LIBBY:	Yeah, it was cool wasn't it? He was cute as a pup dressed up like that. I can tell you, little Cody was the life of the party. I can't wait 'til Halloween.
SAM:	No! You're not going to make my son into some freak show to entertain your pot-smoking, liquor-drinking friends.
LIBBY:	Dude, I'm telling you to chill out, okay? Cody enjoyed himself. He's my son too, you know, mister born-again Christian.
SAM:	He is just a child. He doesn't understand what's going on, but I *do*. Trust me, I'm not going to just stand by and let you ruin him. If you can't agree to that, then I'm going to have to take you to court.
LIBBY:	Aw, dude, are you threatening me? Wow! We used to be so cool back in the day—you know, before you started spouting all this holier-than-thou mumbo jumbo.

SAM:	That was then, and this is now. If you don't come out of this hippie, wild child funk you're in, you're going to need a good lawyer. I'm serious.
LIBBY:	You know what? I thought Christians were all about love, but right now you ain't showing me no love, baby. Right now you're blowing my high; but high or no high, you ain't getting Cody. I'm his mama. I gave him life. Are you feeling me? Now you dig that, mister born again.

What do we say? Did Sam overreact? Was he too harsh and unchristian? Isn't marijuana accepted now in most social circles? Was there anything wrong with Cody dressing up as a girl? When he threatened to take Libby to court, did Sam act from love or fear? Discuss.

What does the *Word* say? Read scriptures from: James 1:5, 3:13; Ephesians 5:8–17; Luke 21:14–15; 1 Corinthians 6:1–6, 13:4–8, 15:33; Romans 12:2, 14–21; Proverbs 5:3–6, 22:6; 1 Peter 3:15–16; and Matthew 5:16, 10:14.

Determine which scriptures apply to each person involved in this case. Can you think of any scriptures to add? In the notes section below, write down your preferred scripture regarding this situation. Memorize it.

Notes

_____

_____

_____

_____

_____

_____

_____

_____

_____

_____

Session 11

Tammy Wants a Husband

Tammy had grown up in church. She had been a Christian for twenty of her thirty-two years. She had a good job at the Christian bookstore but would trade it in a second for a husband. She had four older sisters who were already married, but she didn't even have a boyfriend. She longed to be married with a family of her own. However, God hadn't sent her a husband yet. Week after week she met a variety of men at her job, but she felt that she was too shy, too plain, and too overweight to hold a man's attention for very long. She had never had an intimate relationship with a man in all her life, though in her fantasies she was everything any man would ever want.

Tammy's favorite form of escapism was reading historical romance novels. She first started reading them when she turned nineteen. The language in the books was often graphic and sexually explicit, but she continued to read them. Generally after reading a book, she closed her eyes and fantasized about being the heroine in the romantic novel she'd just finished. Her fantasizing had become so intense that she had sought more satisfaction on Internet porn sites.

After visiting those sites, she would instantly feel guilty and depressed. She tried to stop, but she couldn't break herself from either reading the books or going to the websites. Each would bring her temporary pleasure but shortly afterward guilt, shame, and depression. Part of her wanted to stop the cycle, but part of her also felt empty and alone without some type of sexual gratification.

FACILITATOR:	Role it and action!
TINA:	Tammy, what's the matter? Why are you looking so down? Sunday dinner at my house is supposed to be fun!
TAMMY:	It's the same old thing.
TINA:	What's that? Oh, yeah, no man and no young'uns of your own. Is that what it is again?
TAMMY:	Ha, ha! I know I'm a big joke to you and the rest of the family, but I'm thirty-two years old, and I want to hold my own baby in my arms. I want my own husband. It's hard being single and a Christian. I feel so lonely at times.
TINA:	Child, it's hard being *married* and a Christian, and if it seems like we're making fun of you, I'm sorry. But honestly, you probably could have had a family of your own by now if you had stopped reading all those dirty books. You could've been *living* life instead of fantasizing about it.
TAMMY:	How did you know that I was doing those things?
TINA:	Girl, back in the day, we all read those kinds of books until the Holy Spirit brought us under conviction. Once we turned that stuff loose, God started blessing us.
TAMMY:	What do you mean?
TINA:	I mean if you really want a family of your own, first, you need to repent from those stubborn sins.
TAMMY:	What are stubborn sins?
TINA:	You know what I mean. They're the sins we cling to and don't want to give up such as lusting, fantasizing, watching dirty movies, overeating, overspending, and those kinds of things. Replace those sins and bad habits with praying, fasting, exercise, eating right, volunteering, and Bible study.
TAMMY:	I never thought about it that way. Do you know as long as I've been a Christian I've never fasted? Does it really help?

What do we say? What are some reasons why Tammy has never fasted? Is fasting more about giving up pleasure or is it about repentance over sins? Why do you suppose Tammy felt guilt about fantasizing? Is it okay to fantasize sexually? Why do you think romance novels and soap operas are considered soft pornography? What are other ways singles deal with loneliness? Discuss.

What does the *Word* say? Read scriptures from: Isaiah 40:28–31; Psalms 27:13–14; Ecclesiastes 4:9–12; Hebrews 13:5; 1 Corinthians 6:18, 7:1–2, 10:13; 1 Peter 5:6–9; Romans 12:2; Matthew 6:16–18; James 1:14–15; 2 Timothy 2:22; Philippians 4:8; Ephesians 1:16–19; and James 4:7-10.

Determine which scriptures apply to each person involved in this case. Can you think of any scriptures to add? In the notes section below, write down your preferred scripture regarding this situation. Memorize it.

Notes

_____
_____
_____
_____
_____
_____
_____
_____
_____
_____
_____

Session 12

Felix—Honoring the Onerous

Felix was sexually abused by his father for eight years. His father molested him from the time he was four until he was twelve. The abuse did not stop until he and his mother were finally able to get away. His older brother, Harold,[1] had left home at age seventeen, long before Felix was a teenager. No one in the family had seen or heard from him since. Though their mother inquired with the authorities regarding Harold's whereabouts, Harold was never located. Felix and his mother moved away to another state. He did not know what had happened to his father or brother and never thought he'd see them again. He had been given another chance, and all he wanted to do was put his past behind him and get on with his life.

In their new home, Felix had come home early one afternoon. He heard his mother crying and sobbing in her room. He saw her on her knees by her bed with the Bible open. She then looked up at him and repeated over and over that she was sorry. He turned away, unable to say anything to her. After that day, they went to church each Sunday.

Six years later, he enrolled in college, and through the kindness of a church member, he learned of an internship program in the field of criminal justice. Felix loved the law and graduated summa cum laude. His mother died a year after he graduated from college. He went on to become a lawyer and developed a reputation for being the best at putting pedophiles and rapists behind bars.

---

[1] See Harold's story in session 24.

Because of the things that happened in his childhood, Felix received counseling for many years. He still struggled with sexual intimacy and opted to stay single. God had helped him get over the hurt and hatred he felt toward his biological father. He had equally healed from the anger and bitterness he'd felt toward his mother. Through it all, he'd learned to be content with what he had.

Through work, church, and sports, Felix found satisfaction in life. Work and church kept him busy enough. He didn't need more from life. He felt happiest when he taught adult Bible study. He believed the Bible to be infallible and inerrant. However, a phone call from a social worker changed all he had ever believed about his faith and the Bible.

FACILITATOR:	Role it and action!
SOCIAL WORKER:	Mr. Blake? Mr. Felix Blake? We have a sixty-six-year-old man here at our facility named Horace Blake who says you're his son. Is that correct?
FELIX:	Excuse me? What did you say?
SOCIAL WORKER:	Your father, Horace, is sick, and we are planning to admit him at Metro Community Hospital in a few minutes. He has double pneumonia and a number of other complications that will have to be addressed *when* and *if* he is released from the hospital. We don't have any more room to house him here at our facility.
FELIX:	I'm sorry, but how did you get this number?
SOCIAL WORKER:	Your father listed you as his next of kin, and we were able to find you from there.
FELIX:	I see.
SOCIAL WORKER:	Mr. Blake, your father will need a place to stay once he comes from the hospital. Can we put your address down as his place of residence?

What do we say? How should Felix answer the social worker? Should he take his estranged father in under his roof? Is it possible that God would ask him to take in a man who had once sexually abused him? Could you do it? What are some alternatives for Felix? Discuss.

What does the *Word* say? Read scriptures from: Exodus 21:17; Matthew 5:43–48, 24:12–13; Luke 17:1–4; Romans 12:17–21, 8:28–30; Mark 11:25; Ephesians 4:31–32; Proverbs 3:5–8; 1 Timothy 5:8; and John 14:26.

Determine which scriptures apply to each person involved in this case. Can you think of any scriptures to add? In the notes section below, write down your preferred scripture regarding this situation. Memorize it.

Notes

_____

_____

_____

_____

_____

_____

_____

_____

_____

_____

Session 13

Jennifer—Deflecting the Darts of a Devil

Jennifer had recently lost her husband. She went to stay with her daughter's family out of town for a while before returning home. Her house was a beautiful showplace, but she felt restless in it after her husband's death. It no longer felt like home. She thought of putting it up for sale but needed more advice on how to initiate the process. She and her husband were at retirement age when he died, and Jennifer dreaded being in the house all day with nothing to do.

The following week, she started volunteering at her favorite charity along with attending church functions more frequently. She joined the senior usher board and the mass choir. She alternated each week to accommodate both functions. One Tuesday evening, while waiting for the ushers' meeting to start, she asked one of her fellow ushers, Mr. Jones, about selling her house. He had years of real estate experience and knew the ins and outs of the process. He promised to call or drop by with the necessary information and winked at her in a flirtatious manner. Needless to say, Jennifer hadn't answered his call. He eventually stopped leaving messages and never mentioned it to her again.

Soon after that incident, she began to notice many others from certain men in the church. On several occasions, men said inappropriate things to her, touched her in inappropriate ways, stared at her lewdly, and spoke to her suggestively without any provocation on her part. It would have been laughable if it had only stopped there.

One night after choir rehearsal as she walked to her car, a choir member came up beside her. He told a joke that was coarse and degrading. When she didn't laugh, he became angry and said she was pretending to be uppity but he knew she liked things dirty. She threatened to tell his wife about his behavior, and he laughed. He told her nobody would believe a desperate widow over an upstanding family man. He threatened to let everyone know that it was *she* who had come on to him. Jennifer was appalled and shaken by what he said. She was so upset that she cried herself to sleep that night. The reality of being alone and unprotected frightened her in a way she hadn't felt in a long time. She knew she had done nothing wrong, but she felt somehow at fault. She missed the comfort of her husband's arms and his broad shoulders to lean on.

FACILITATOR:	Role it and action!
DENISE:	Hello, Jennifer, this is Denise at the church. We've missed you at choir rehearsal. Are you feeling okay?
JENNIFER:	To be honest, I'm not sure how I feel, Denise.
DENISE:	Jennifer, do you mind if I speak to you frankly as a friend?
JENNIFER:	Yes, go ahead.
DENISE:	Well, I think I know who kept you from coming back to choir rehearsal. I just want you to know that you're not the only woman in the choir who has been insulted by that creep.
JENNIFER:	How do you know what happened?
DENISE:	Someone overheard what he said to you in the church parking lot and shared the information with me after you stopped coming to church.
JENNIFER:	Hallelujah! I'm so glad someone else heard him and saw that I wasn't some desperate, lonely old woman trying to tempt a virtuous married man.
DENISE:	Welcome to the world of single and widowed women everywhere. A lot of men think we're fair game. They believe that they have the right to say things to us that are inappropriate, even in church settings.
JENNIFER:	But why, when we haven't asked for their attention?

DENISE:	I don't know why. When my Harry died, three of his deacon buddies tried to come on to me, and Harry hadn't been dead a year. One of them was extremely lecherous, and he was married to a friend of mine! I feel sorry for his poor wife.
JENNIFER:	But I never thought Christian men would behave this way in church, and I have not encouraged any of them. I'm still grieving over my husband for goodness sake.
DENISE:	I know, and I'm sorry this happened to you, but you can't go around any longer thinking just because you're widowed that you're safe. You have to put on the whole armor of God. As an unmarried woman, you no longer have the protection of your husband. That's why we single ladies travel in pairs and bunches. Trust me, it's a lot safer.
JENNIFER:	I guess I've been pretty naïve about things but it's been so long since I was single. I'll have to be reprogrammed on how to stay safe and single in a church setting.
DENISE:	It does take some adjusting, but I've talked to the pastor and several key deacons about it. They are going to meet with this man and address his offensive behavior so that, prayerfully, it won't happen again.
JENNIFER:	That's good news.
DENISE:	Yes, it is. You may receive a phone call from one of the deacons in a few days to tell your side of what happened. Are you comfortable with that?
JENNIFER:	I sure am.
DENISE:	Good. So, are you planning to come back to choir rehearsal?
JENNIFER:	Yes, I'm coming back.
DENISE:	Well, praise the Lord! I'll come by and pick you up.

What do we say? Do you think Jennifer should have laughed at the joke and dismissed the entire incident? Why was she frightened by what happened? Should the coarse joker's wife be informed about her husband's behavior?

Do you think these kinds of things happen all the time and women simply don't discuss them? Why do you think women remain silent about inappropriate behavior in a church setting? Discuss.

What does the *Word* say? Read scriptures from: Psalm 68:5–6; Proverbs 6:12–14, 15:25; 1 Thessalonians 4:7–8; Ephesians 5:11–12; Hebrews 12:14–15; and James 1:2–4.

Determine which scriptures apply to each person involved in this case. Can you think of any scriptures to add? In the notes section below, write down your preferred scripture regarding this situation. Memorize it.

Notes

_____
_____
_____
_____
_____
_____
_____
_____
_____
_____

Session 14

Connie's Money's Funny

Connie was drowning! She struggled to stay afloat financially each day. Her three kids, ages fourteen, ten, and six, had an ever-growing list of things they needed. All three of them needed tutors and new shoes. Her oldest needed money for the school field trip coming up next Tuesday. Her middle child needed a good winter coat, and the youngest needed ear tubes due to constant infections. Her insurance would only pay so much. The rest would have to come out of her pocket. She didn't know where she was going to get the money for the tubes or anything else on the list. She constantly felt guilty because she never seemed to have enough money or time for her children. She only spent about an hour a day with them during the week because she worked the second shift. They needed her, and she needed approximately two weeks of uninterrupted sleep.

She saw no immediate way of getting any of what they needed. The children's father had run out on her during her third pregnancy, and she hadn't been able to track him down for child support. She knew if she moved back home she could get help with her kids from her family. She missed their support terribly and talked to them long-distance nearly every day. She regretted that she had moved away when she'd first gotten married to her husband, but after he abandoned her, she couldn't afford to move back home. In fact, there were no big job opportunities in her hometown anyway. Besides, she didn't want to uproot her children. It wouldn't be fair to them, and they'd been through enough.

She had prayed many times for God to help. She had the women at church to pray for her too. Many of the ladies at her church promised to plan for support groups, tutors, and after-school programs for single parents. It was earmarked in their long-term budget planning. They agreed that all the programs were great ideas, but three years had passed, and no progress had been made. They had collected a love offering for her during the Christmas holidays last year, and Connie had been grateful. Unfortunately, what she needed couldn't be fixed with a Christmas donation. She needed ongoing help.

FACILITATOR:	Role it and action!
EDNA:	Oh, my goodness, is that you, Connie? I barely recognized you. You look a hot mess! Look at your hair and your eyes. I could sleep in those bags under your eyes. Oh, my poor baby sister. What's happened to you?
CONNIE:	It's good to see you too, Edna. It's great that you don't visit too often because I don't think I could bear any more of your praise.
EDNA:	Very funny. I'm certainly not here to criticize you. I'm here with some good news.
CONNIE:	I've inherited millions of dollars.
EDNA:	I wish! How about a free afternoon program for the kids instead?
CONNIE:	Free? Whatchu talkin' 'bout, Willis?
EDNA:	My name isn't Willis, but yes, it's free. They also have something called the open closet. It's where church members can get gently used clothes and shoes for free.
CONNIE:	Where is this church?
EDNA:	On South Main Street. It's called the New Community Church. It's the church where Jesus lives. That's what it says on their sign. I saw it when I was coming off the interstate.
CONNIE:	I vaguely remember hearing about that church, but I didn't know they did all that over there. Since I sleep in the morning and work at night, I don't know half of what's going on in the world.

EDNA:	Apparently you don't know what's going on in your own city. Anyway, I stopped and got a brochure. The people were really very friendly. This older lady named Penny told me they're big on community outreach. Their programs are for all members of their church body, especially widows and single moms. I saw a couple of good-looking guys over there too.
CONNIE:	It's *that* kind of thinking that landed me with three kids.
EDNA:	Sorry, I got off track. Anyway, Penny said they provide free health screenings and after-school programs. Oh, and they offer computer classes too.
CONNIE:	I'm impressed! I've been looking for this kind of outreach for about three years.
EDNA:	I know you have. You've tithed at your church, you've been faithful in helping where you could, and you've supported the pastor. Three years have gone by, and you haven't received the help you've needed as a single mother, yet.
CONNIE:	No, I haven't, have I?

What do you say? Should Connie continue to wait, or should she move her membership to get the support she needs? Do you think most churches are sensitive to the needs of single-parent families, widows, and divorced individuals? Why or why not? Discuss.

What does the *Word* say? Read scriptures from: Isaiah 55:1, 58:6–7, 30:18; Proverbs 21:13; Leviticus 25:35–36; Psalm 41:1; 1 Timothy 5:8; 1 John 3:17–18; Galatians 6:9–10; Matthew 11:28-30, 25:37–40; Philippians 2:4–5; and James 2:14–16.

Determine which scriptures apply to each person involved in this case. Can you think of any scriptures to add? In the notes section below, write down your preferred scripture regarding this situation. Memorize it.

Notes

_____

_____

_____

Annette Richardson

Session 15

John—Love Me, Love My Son

John was a forty-four-year-old widower with a mentally challenged adult son named Otis. John had some health issues of his own, including high blood pressure and diabetes. He worried what would happen if he died before Otis. He prayed God would take care of his son.

John wanted to marry again but wondered if it was selfish to think of saddling a woman with a mentally challenged son and a would-be spouse with chronic health issues. He had only gone out on two dates since his wife, Linda, died three years ago. Both dates had ended poorly once they met his son. Otis was twenty-three years old and would always need someone to look after him. John sent his son to an adult daycare while he worked. After work and on weekends, he cared for his son solely.

John missed his wife terribly. When she was alive, they went to church, went to movies, and did numerous things as a family. When she died, members of his church stopped coming around. He missed the fellowship. He was therefore elated when he met Shelley. She worked in the same health care clinic where his endocrinologist's office was located. Shelley was a nurse, and during their conversation over lunch, he found out that she was a warm and compassionate woman. She fully understood the complexities of diabetes and high blood pressure and didn't seem to have a problem with his health issues. Emboldened by her kindness, John asked Shelley over to his house for dinner Saturday night. Shelley agreed.

John found himself thinking of Shelley all week. Two hours before the dinner date, he called Shelley and told her about Otis being mentally challenged. Shelley sounded distracted but said that it didn't bother her at all that his son was mentally challenged. She then expressed deep regret at having to forgo their dinner date. She had to work overtime that weekend. She would call him when she was free to have dinner.

FACILITATOR:	Role it and action!
JOHN:	Hey, Shelley, this is John. How are you?
SHELLEY:	Oh, hello John. To tell you the truth I'm swamped. How are you?
JOHN:	I'm fine. I'm doing fine. So, you're really busy, huh?
SHELLEY:	Yes, I am. It's the flu season and we're always very busy during this time of year.
JOHN:	Yeah, sure, I understand. I just called because it's been a week since I last heard from you, but I'll let you go since you're bogged down right now.
SHELLEY:	Yes, I'm terribly sorry. Maybe I can give you a call next week and we can get together again.
JOHN:	Yeah, sure, you give me a call.
SHELLEY:	Okay, I'll talk to you real soon. Take care, bye.
JOHN:	Bye.

What do we say? Should John believe Shelley? Why or why not? Should a parent date someone who can't accept his or her child? Do you think John ever resents his son, Otis? Is Shelley wrong if she doesn't want to get involved with John because of his son? Why or why not? What are some things John could do to improve his situation? Discuss.

What does the *Word* say? Read scriptures from: Psalms 25:1, 16–18, 28:7, 34:18, 55:22, 103:13–14,17–18; Lamentations 3:24–26, 31–33, 55–57; 1 Corinthians 13:4–7; 2 Corinthians 12:8–10; Galatians 6:2; Philippians 4:4–7; Matthew 11:28–30; Romans 15:13, 8:18, 28; and 1 Peter 5:6–7.

Determine which scriptures apply to each person involved in this case. Can you think of any scriptures to add? In the notes section below, write down your preferred scripture regarding this situation. Memorize it.

Notes

_____

_____

_____

_____
_____
_____
_____
_____
_____
_____
_____
_____
_____
_____
_____
_____
_____
_____
_____
_____
_____
_____

Session 16

Jessica—Diffusing a Bombshell

Jessica was a dangerously beautiful, single girl who was new in the faith. She was also a new member of the All Saints Holy Community Church. Jessica had just turned eighteen years old and was known for dressing provocatively when she attended Sunday morning worship service. Her parents were also new members at the church. They were lawyers by profession, with very progressive views and ideas. Each Sunday morning when Jessica walked down the aisle to find a seat, several pairs of male eyes followed her to her destination with very *unholy* interest. While Jessica used the church aisle as her own personal catwalk, she drew several pairs of female eyes with very unholy interest as well—though not for the same unholy reasons.

Jessica was a babe (immature) in Christ and still had some very carnal ideas about life. Jessica's fashion sense and beauty were very popular among young people in the church. Many younger teenage girls tried to copy Jessica's style. Jessica had become quite a distraction. She was such a constant distraction that congregational tongues were wagging about her each Sunday morning. Some people were afraid of the carnal influence Jessica had on young girls at the church. Some people were more afraid of the carnal influence Jessica had on young *boys* at the church. Some people were most afraid of Jessica's parents, who might file a lawsuit against the church. If the pastor preached a sermon against Jessica's style of dress, the pastor could be liable for spouting hate speech. Jessica was a dangerously beautiful single girl indeed.

FACILITATOR:	Role it and action!
CHURCH WOMAN 1:	Did you see what that little hoochie mama was wearing today? It was *scandalous*! How can her parents allow her to come out of the house dressed that way?
CHURCH WOMAN 2:	Honey, I don't know, but I thought my husband's eyes were going to pop right out of his bald head.
CHURCH WOMAN 3:	It's shameful, and this has to stop. People are more interested in what Jessica is wearing on Sundays than they are in hearing God's Word.
CHURCH WOMAN 1:	You've got that right. My daughter came down the stairs Friday night with face paint on as thick as molasses and said, "It's what Jessica wears." What? I went berserk.
CHURCH WOMAN 2:	My sixteen-year-old son comes to church now more than he ever has, and all he says is, "Jessie's hot, man. Jessie's hot!" It makes me want to puke!
CHURCH WOMAN 3:	Why doesn't the pastor *do* something or *say* something to stop this madness?
CHURCH WOMAN 1:	I think he's worried about what her parents might try to do to the church. There's some talk that Jessica's parents won a boatload of money in a lawsuit for a transvestite in the church they attended before coming to All Saints.
CHURCH WOMAN 2:	Is that true? You don't think they would try to sue us, do you? I thought they were from Canada.
CHURCH WOMAN 3:	In this state, it could be misconstrued as hate speech if the pastor talked against dress styles. In any case, they could call in the media and make trouble for our church.
CHURCH WOMAN 1:	Well, somebody has got to do something because things with this girl are getting out of control.

CHURCH WOMAN 2:   *We* need to do something. I'm going to ask the pastor's wife to call a meeting with the women of the church.

CHURCH WOMAN 3:   Yes, ladies, and we need to pray.

What do we say? Does Jessica have the right to dress provocatively in church? Doesn't a woman have a right to wear what she wishes? Should the pastor step in? How should Jessica and her family be handled? Should Christians sue Christians? Are Biblical truths considered hate speech? What does the Bible say about speaking the truth? Discuss.

What does the *Word* say? Read scriptures from: 1 Peter 1:14–16, 2:1–3; Romans 8:5–8, 12:1, 16:17–18; 2 Peter 2:1–3; Proverbs 31:30, 7:10; Revelation 2:20; 1 Timothy 2:9–10; 1 Corinthians 6:1–8; James 2:8–9, 3:9–11, 4:7–8; Titus 2:3–5; Matthew 18:15–17; and Philippians 1:27–28.

Determine which scriptures apply to each person involved in this case. Can you think of any scriptures to add? In the notes section below, write down your preferred scripture regarding this situation. Memorize it.

Notes

_____

_____

_____

_____

_____

_____

_____

_____

_____

_____

_____

_____

_____

_____

_____

_____

Session 17

The Preacher's Pride

Pastor Justin Connors found that the current state of affairs in his life read like a segment taken from an O. Henry novel. His critics might say justice was served at last, but he could not appreciate the irony of the situation. The shame and embarrassment of his recent divorce was by far the most humiliating experience in his life to date. His ex-wife filed for divorce and claimed irreconcilable differences as the reason for the marriage's demise. The news of his divorce had made the local papers because of his near-celebrity status as a pro-marriage, pro-family crusader. In his zeal, he accumulated thousands of supporters who sent money to further his ministry.

His radio and televised sermons in the past had been fiery discourses preached with passion and conviction against the divorce pandemic that had swept through the nation. He had boldly proclaimed that the selfishness of adultery, the weakness of fornication, and perversion of homosexuality were the leading causes of divorce. He had been a strong advocate of the sanctity of marriage and had never cheated on his wife. He had expounded on divorce not ever being an option for God's people. Yet in his case, his wife had left him no choice but to be an unwilling party to what he considered prodigious sin. No amount of begging and pleading on his part had changed her mind. His wife wanted a divorce.

Because of his fervent campaigning against divorce, he had sensed the word *hypocrite* poised on the collective lips of his congregational members. As they watched him step into the pulpit each Sunday morning, he knew that much of his credibility as a pastor had been lost. How could God allow him to be exposed in this disgraceful way when he'd always stood up fiercely for the sanctity of marriage?

FACILITATOR:	Role it and action!
JIMMY:	Hello, Justin. How are you? Don't answer. I can tell by your expression things are pretty bad.
PASTOR:	You're right about that, and since I'm a pastor, there are only a few people I can turn to when I need a sounding board. You're one of my oldest friends, so you're it.
JIMMY:	Go ahead and let it out.
PASTOR:	It's this thing with Wilma and the divorce. I mean, I don't understand why God would allow me to go through something like this when He knows how much I love my wife. I love my children and my grandchildren. I have honored my marriage vows. I can't understand it. Why am I going through this?
JIMMY:	I know you tried to make things right with Wilma, but she basically made you choose between her and the ministry. It was a hard choice, but you chose the ministry.
PASTOR:	I still wrestle with whether I made the right decision. I could have retired and spent my life writing. I could have ministered to people through my books. I chose the pulpit as my heart's desire and all that goes with it. Perhaps she couldn't forgive me for making that choice.
JIMMY:	Is that the only thing bothering you?
PASTOR:	That's just the tip of the iceberg. The other stuff that's hard to take is the gloating from others, the judging, and the idea that I'm a hypocrite. It's the letters in the mail that read, "I told you so." It's almost too much to bear some days.
JIMMY:	I hear you but I would like to ask you something that goes a little deeper. Do you think God is trying to show you something in all of this? Do you ever think that in the past

you came off as self-righteous or proud when you preached against divorce? I know this may seem harsh, but do you think your marriage was an idol to you? Is it more your pride that's hurting right now than anything else?

What do we say? What are some reasons even the best of Christian marriages fail? Do we judge divorced people too harshly in the church body? Why was the pastor angry with God? Were there other options for the pastor's ministry besides preaching from the pulpit? Was his friend Jimmy right to have him examine his hurt more closely? Discuss.

What does the *Word* say? Read scriptures from: James 4:6,10; Matthew 23:12, 7:1–2; Ephesians 2:8–9, 4:2, 32; Romans 3:23, 8:18, 28; Proverbs; 16:18; Psalms 34:18, 73:26; Isaiah 41:20; Lamentations 3:22–23; 2 Timothy 4:2, 5; John 21:15; and Mark 11:25.

Determine which scriptures apply to each person involved in this case. Can you think of any scriptures to add? In the notes section below, write down your preferred scripture regarding this situation. Memorize it.

Notes

_____

_____

_____

_____

_____

_____

_____

_____

_____

_____

Session 18

Distinguishing and Extinguishing God's Gifts

Morgan studied the Bible since childhood and seemed to have a gift for explaining and expounding on the scriptures. The older Morgan became, the more her gift was manifested. Kyle, Morgan's older brother, was encouraged by their parents to preach and to go seminary, but they encouraged Morgan to go to college and become an elementary school teacher.

Neither sibling followed their parents' advice for a vocation. Eventually Kyle dropped out of seminary and went on to teach mathematics in the public school system, while Morgan went to the mission fields, feeling compelled to preach the gospel. Nearly ten years later, Morgan died on the mission field in Africa during a severe political uprising that took the lives of 231 people. Her body was shipped back home, where her parents, Robert and Frieda, grieved the loss of their only daughter and the awful way that she died in a pagan society.

FACILITATOR: Role it and action!
ROBERT: For God's sake, Frieda Mae, stop throwing all
            those reproachful looks toward me, will you?
            Don't you think I feel bad enough?
FRIEDA: We should have encouraged Morgan to become
            a preacher right here in the United States.
            Maybe she'd still be alive if we had.

ROBERT:	You can't say that for sure.
FRIEDA:	Well, I would feel better if we hadn't been so bigoted about our own daughter becoming a preacher.
ROBERT:	We're not bigots. Our church just doesn't recognize women preachers. Our daughter would have been a freak. No one would have taken her seriously. Preaching and pastoring are men's work. Women need to accept that's the way God intended it to be and that's that!
FRIEDA:	How do we know? Morgan had the gift of preaching ever since she was a child. If God didn't give it to her, where did it come from?
ROBERT:	I'm not going to discuss this any longer, Frieda Mae. A woman has her place, and it is not competing with a man to be a preacher! For all we know she could have died because of her disobedience to the Word.

What do we say? Do children exhibit spiritual gifts at an early age? What is your spiritual gift? Are all *men* qualified to teach and preach the Word of God? Why do some denominations encourage women to preach the gospel and others do not? Is it biblical for women to preach the gospel? What *exactly* does the Bible say? Discuss.

What does the *Word* say? Read scriptures from: Joel 2:28–29; Matthew 10:39; 1 Corinthians 14:33–35; 1 Timothy 2:11–14; 1 Peter 2:13–17, 5:6–9; James 3:1–2; 2 Thessalonians 2:14–15; Acts 4:12; John 3:36; Romans 3:27–28; and Psalm 29:11.

Determine which scriptures apply to each person involved in this case. Can you think of any scriptures to add? In the notes section below, write down your preferred scripture regarding this situation. Memorize it.

Notes

_____

_____

_____

_____

_____

_____

Scenarios for Singles

_____
_____
_____
_____
_____
_____
_____
_____
_____
_____

Session 19

Joanne's Vicious Cycle

Joanne was the oldest of nine children. She helped her mother raise her brothers and sisters after her father was shot by a jealous husband. Joanne's mother worked as a domestic in private homes and a cook in public schools. At age fifteen, Joanne ran off to marry a man seventeen years her senior. She had gotten tired of living in her mother's house like a slave, doing as she was told with no freedom. Her goal was to have her own husband, her own home, and her own children.

After fifteen years of marriage, Joanne's husband, Grady, died from a massive heart attack, leaving her alone to raise three daughters. He had also left behind a considerable amount of debt to be paid off. At age thirty, Joanne entered the work force as a domestic helper, cleaning private homes and public schools. She worked from sun up to sun down five days a week and half days on Saturdays and Sundays. Within five years of her husband's death, her oldest daughter had a child out of wedlock. Her second daughter was seeing a man old enough to be her father. Her youngest daughter was following in her oldest sister's footsteps. She was doing drugs and was four months pregnant by a married man.

Joanne felt overwhelmed. When she wasn't working, she cared for her grandson. His mother would then go off for hours to God knew where. She couldn't get her daughters to help with the bills, groceries, or anything worthwhile. They didn't care. She had no one to help her. When she woke up in the mornings, she was tired. When she went to bed, she was tired and alone. She wondered if things would ever change in her life.

FACILITATOR:	Role it and action!
FRIEND:	Joanne, why are you riding the bus today?
JOANNE:	I missed my ride this morning because I was running late.
FRIEND:	If you don't mind my saying so, you look tired enough to fall off this seat.
JOANNE:	I am tired. I've been tired all my life.
FRIEND:	Why do you say that?
JOANNE:	I raised my mama's children, I raised my own children, I buried my husband, and now I'm raising my grandson.
FRIEND:	I heard that your youngest is doing eleven to twenty-nine in the county jail.
JOANNE:	Yeah, I'm tired of her too.
FRIEND:	Joanne, I was wondering if I could ask you something personal.
JOANNE:	What is it?
FRIEND:	Do you have a personal relationship with Jesus? I mean, have you ever asked Him to come into your life and save you?
JOANNE:	No, I never thought any of that religious stuff or Jesus could help me.
FRIEND:	Yes, He can!
JOANNE:	How do you know He can help me?
FRIEND:	I know because He helped me. I was so burdened down before Jesus came into my life.
JOANNE:	That's exactly how I feel. How did Jesus help you? What did you have to do?

What do we say? Do you know any grandparents who have raised their children and are now having to raise their grandchildren? Do you think they're tired and would appreciate some help? Name some problems passed down through generations. Why do you suppose these same problems keep showing up? When was the last time you shared your faith with an older person? Discuss.

What does the *Word* say? Read scriptures from: Isaiah 30:18; Matthew 5:8, 11:28–30, 16:24–27, 28:19; Mark 16:15–16; Luke 15:7; John 3:16–17; 1 Peter 3:15; Romans 1:16–17, 5:6–8, 8:6–9, 10:8–11, 17; 2 Corinthians 1:4, 7:10; 1 Timothy 1:15; and Jude 1:22.

Determine which scriptures apply to each person involved in this case. Can you think of any scriptures to add? In the notes section below, write down your preferred scripture regarding this situation. Memorize it.

Notes

_____

_____

_____

_____

_____

_____

_____

_____

_____

_____

Session 20

Tony and a Taste of Vinegar

Tony knew Allyson was young. In fact, she was twenty-one years his junior and he didn't care. She was a fine, sweet, Christian girl who said she loved him, and he believed her. He loved her too and planned to ask her to marry him. She was outgoing, open, and liked his jokes. He shrugged off the rumors that she only liked him for his money. As it turned out, her family was quite wealthy.

He was concerned that their age difference would be a problem with her parents. They were the same age. He got along well with her father, but her mother treated him coolly. It was the typical response from women his age. It was the same way with older women at his church when they saw him with Allyson. He couldn't understand why they were judging him. He hadn't broken any law, but middle-aged women seemed to be angry about his relationship with Allyson. Didn't they understand that their attitude was part of the reason he'd started dating a younger woman in the first place?

FACILITATOR:	Role it and action!
BARBARA:	Daddy?
TONY:	Yes, sweetheart.
BARBARA:	You know that I *like* Allyson, right?
TONY:	Yes, but what's on your mind? You seem to be a little upset.

BARBARA:	Well, to tell you the truth, it's embarrassing to see my own father going around with a child who could be my younger sister.
TONY:	Allyson *is* young, but she is not a child. Why is it embarrassing to *you*?
BARBARA:	Do you even have to ask? People are talking about it, *and* I think it's a disgrace to Mom's memory. She was a beautiful woman in her early forties who died too young but who lived with dignity.
TONY:	Your mother was indeed a very beautiful and dignified woman, sweetheart, but she wasn't forty when I met her.
BARBARA:	What's that supposed to mean?
TONY:	It means after your mother's death, I began to date again. I started out with women around my age, but as I got to know them, things got a little weird.
BARBARA:	*Weird?*
TONY:	Let's just say that many of my experiences with these ladies were pretty negative. They seemed angry, bitter, suspicious, and extremely defensive.
BARBARA:	C'mon, Daddy, all of them?
TONY:	Yes, even that *sweet* Mrs. Greene you set me up with to take out to dinner. Did I mention sarcastic?
BARBARA:	Mrs. Greene? She's never been sarcastic with me. She's always so sweet.
TONY:	Sweet? Oh, no, she definitely has the taste of vinegar on her tongue. She's the one who snarled at me, "Thank you, but I can pay for my own dinner. That way I know there won't be any hanky-panky afterwards. Here's a dollar. I can use that plus my ex-husband's alimony check to tip the waiter."
BARBARA:	(Laughing.) She said that?
TONY:	I'm sorry to break it to you, darling, but yes she said that and a whole lot more. She is one of the reasons I'm now in a relationship with Allyson.

BARBARA:	Are you sure, Daddy? I mean, what on earth do you and Allyson have in common?
TONY:	Whatever we have, it's working. Allyson knows you can catch more flies with honey.

What do we say? Do older divorced women seem bitter? If so, are they justified in behaving suspiciously toward men? How does a person get past the hurt and bitterness from a failed marriage? What are some things a younger person may have to face when marrying a much-older spouse? Did Tony look for any excuse to date a younger woman? Does the old adage, "You can catch more flies with honey" still apply nowadays? Discuss.

What does the *Word* say? Read scriptures from: Proverbs 14:1, 15:13, 18:21; Ruth 1:20–21, 2:13–16, 3:9–11; Matthew 7:1; Mark 7:20–22; Romans 14:10–13; 1 Corinthians 7:8–9; and James 2:12–13.

Determine which scriptures apply to each person involved in this case. Can you think of any scriptures to add? In the notes section below, write down your preferred scripture regarding this situation. Memorize it.

Notes

_____

_____

_____

_____

_____

_____

_____

_____

_____

_____

_____

_____

_____

_____

_____

_____

_____

Session 21

Abortion—the
Deliberate Death

Shawn was deeply depressed. Where was God? He and his girlfriend, Trina, had gotten pregnant. Although his parents taught him sex before marriage was wrong, he and Trina remained sexually active. He didn't really feel guilty because they planned to marry after graduation. Both were juniors in college and had things pretty much planned out. His parents promised to help with the baby so he and Trina could continue to concentrate on school.

Trina caught flak from her parents for getting pregnant. Her father was livid and her mother cried for days after hearing the news. Trina was also very depressed until her mother decided to cheer her up. She came to Trina's room one Thursday night and suggested they go shopping for baby things the next day. She said they would have some girl's day activities and take the whole weekend. She was sure the shopping trip would cheer them up. Her father said he would support any decision they made.

Shawn didn't see Trina during the entire weekend. He called her cell phone and texted, but she wouldn't answer. He wanted to know how she was doing and if the shopping had cheered her up. He called her house that Sunday evening, but her father said Trina couldn't come to the phone. She was studying for her biology exam. For the next few days, Shawn didn't see Trina. He finally caught up with her outside of the campus library.

FACILITATOR:	Role it and action!
SHAWN:	Trina, whoa! Would you wait up? Babe, where are you going in such a hurry? I haven't seen you in forever! Why haven't you answered your phone or any of my texts?
TRINA:	Sorry, but I had to study for my exam. These biology classes are killing me. Look, can we go over by the oak tree and talk where it's quiet?
SHAWN:	Sure, but what's going on? You look so serious.
TRINA:	We're not having the baby.
SHAWN:	We're not having the baby? Why? What happened? Are you all right?
TRINA:	Yes, I'm all right. Would you stop pawing on me? I'm fine.
SHAWN:	I'm sorry, babe. What happened? Why did you say we're not having the baby?
TRINA:	Look, it's over. It's done. There's no baby, okay?
SHAWN:	Over? What do you mean it's over? Did you have some type of accident?
TRINA:	You know what? You are so naïve at times. Mom wanted me to tell you that I lost the baby through a miscarriage but I didn't. I had an abortion, okay?
SHAWN:	You did *what*?
TRINA:	You heard me.
SHAWN:	You *killed* our baby? Who told you to do it? The last time we talked, you never gave the slightest hint that you wanted an abortion. How could you do this without telling me? The baby was mine too, Trina. How could you not make me a part of this?
TRINA:	Oh, my God, are those tears? Are you crying? Listen to me, I had a procedure. That's all it was, a simple procedure.
SHAWN:	It was not just a procedure. You knew that my family and I would have taken the baby if you didn't want it. Instead you went off and did this horrible thing. How could you?

TRINA: Don't you judge me! I don't want to hear that whole, "Thou shalt not kill," thing. My parents have worked too hard for me to go to med school. I can't put my life on hold for a baby right now. I've got med school in front of me.

SHAWN: Trina, don't you understand? I can't share my life with a woman who would do something like this. I just can't. Oh, God, please forgive us for taking the life of an innocent child!

TRINA: You're obviously having a meltdown. You need to stop being so dramatic. It's lame. Women have this procedure done every day. Grow up. It's no big deal!

SHAWN: Are you really this heartless? I can't stand to look at you. I can't believe that I ever said that I loved you.

TRINA: You can't stand to look at *me*? You're the one who's crying. You're so weak and sniveling. You're turning my stomach.

SHAWN: I never want to see you again, Trina.

TRINA: Are you *dumping* me?

What do we say? In cases of abortion, most people think it's a woman's choice, but what about the man's choice or his point of view? What could Shawn have done differently? Trina is a pre-med major and sees abortion simply as a procedure. Is she right? Is an abortion the same as having an appendectomy? What are some reasons women choose abortion? What are some reasons women choose life? Discuss.

What does the *Word* say? Read scriptures from: 1 John 1:9–10, 3:9; Romans 12:2; James 1:15, 4:17; Lamentations 4:3; Psalms 51:1–15, 17, 127:3, 139:13–16; 1 Timothy 4:1–2; Exodus 20:13; Jeremiah 1:5, 22:17; Colossians 2:8; 1 Corinthians 6:19–20; Proverbs 6:16–17, 24:11–12; Ephesians 4:18; Deuteronomy 12:31–32, 30:19; Ezekiel 16:20–21; and Revelation 21:4.

Determine which scriptures apply to each person involved in this case. Can you think of any scriptures to add? In the notes section below, write down your preferred scripture regarding this situation. Memorize it.

Notes

_____

_____

_____

_____

_____

_____

_____

_____

_____

_____

Session 22

Charlie, the Self-Appointed Magistrate

Charlie worked in the same hardware store for nearly twenty-years. He never married and was presently in his mid-forties. He was the oldest son of three siblings, and his parents despaired whether he would ever give them grandchildren or not. He knew he wasn't much to look at to most women. He was short, thin, and balding. He had a nice smile and drew a modest salary. He owned his home, drove a two-year old American-made truck, and lived with a chocolate Labrador retriever named Louie. He believed in God, but he didn't go to church much. The last time he'd gone to church, the preacher seemed way too zealous for his taste. On most Sundays, he preferred fishing to going to church.

However, there were times when he felt lonely. His doctor had prescribed medication for his depression. He'd struggled with feelings of suicide in the past and wondered if God was ever going to take away his loneliness. He wanted a wife and kids, but these days most women wanted a billionaire Adonis, which he was not. His neighbors, Paul and Nina, had promised to set him up with a friend of theirs on the weekend. It was going to be a double date. He prayed that maybe she would be the one. Maybe she would be a nice, godly woman who would go out with an average kind of guy like him.

FACILITATOR: Role it and action!
PAUL: Hey, Charlie, how are you, buddy?

CHARLIE:	I'm okay, I guess.
PAUL:	That's good. Nina asked me to invite you over for dinner after church this afternoon.
CHARLIE:	Is Gloria going to be there?
PAUL:	That's entirely up to you.
CHARLIE:	Yeah, sure, that'll be okay I guess.
PAUL:	What's with all the guessing? I thought you would be walking on clouds today.
CHARLIE:	Why do you say that?
PAUL:	Well, because of your date with Gloria last night. She's a sweet lady, and she really seemed to be into you.
CHARLIE:	Yeah, she was okay. I told her I thought she was nice.
PAUL:	Just nice? Is that your way of saying you didn't really like her?
CHARLIE:	Can I be honest with you, Paul, man to man?
PAUL:	Sure, Charlie.
CHARLIE:	Your wife's friend, Gloria, was not really my type. I mean, she was a nice girl and all. She had a good sense of humor, a cute face, and all of that, but she was too short. You know? She was thick and big-boned. She also looked like she could lose about twenty-five pounds or more. Then I think she said she works as a waitress down at the diner. She can't be making too much money doing that kind of work, can she?
PAUL:	Well, Charlie, maybe you're right about all the things you've said about Gloria. Now can I ask you something, you know, man to man?
CHARLIE:	Shoot.
PAUL:	Couldn't you lower your standards a little and overlook a few of Gloria's flaws? She's really a nice girl, and with all due respect, Charlie, you've got a few flaws too, right? Maybe you should just relax and get to know her. Nobody's asking you to marry her tomorrow. Actually, nobody's asking you to marry her at all!

What do we say? Is Charlie unrealistic in his expectations for a spouse? Do we focus on things that are basically superficial? Are all flaws in another person deal breakers? Do we wonder what our friends or family will say if we choose someone who doesn't meet their expectations? What were some of Charlie's flaws? Discuss.

What does the Word say? Read scriptures from: 1 Corinthians 13:1, 4–7; Galatians 6:3; Romans 14:10, 12, 13; Matthew 7:1–5, 23:12; Proverbs 16:18; and Psalm 37:4.

Determine which scriptures apply to each person involved in this case. Can you think of any scriptures to add? In the notes section below, write down your preferred scripture regarding this situation. Memorize it.

Notes

_____

_____

_____

_____

_____

_____

_____

_____

_____

_____

_____

_____

_____

_____

_____

_____

_____

_____

_____

Session 23

Paula and Great Expectations

Paula was an extremely intelligent and gifted career woman. To the outside world, she exuded poise and wielded purpose. She held a PhD in business finance and was considered one of the best minds in her field. She had been corporate vice president at her company for the past eight years and had written several books on the world of finance. Her awards for her work and civic contributions were impressive symbols of her success to her business colleagues.

Yet for all of her accomplishments, she was not considered a total success in the eyes of her parents. She was their only offspring. Her father was an ex-marine and proud of being an overachiever. He was also proud to have passed those character traits along to his daughter. At her age, she had done well, but he'd expected her to own at least one business. He assumed she'd be married to a doctor, have two perfect children, a purebred dog, and living in a house worth six figures. She had laughed, but deep inside it hurt to know that she had fallen short of his expectations.

Although they were proud of her business acumen, her parents were embarrassed by her single status. Once she'd overheard her mother tell a friend that it seemed her daughter would never find a husband or have children. If she'd gotten married twenty years ago without a penny, why couldn't her daughter marry with everything going for her? Even though she was a toughened businesswoman, Paula was wounded by her mother's remarks. It was a blow to her self-esteem to know that all her achievements meant nothing to her family since she was not married with children.

If she was honest, she would admit that there were times when she didn't feel like a great success either. She realized that it was not only the way *others* viewed her that made her so unhappy but wrestling with her own inner demons as well. Her feelings of fear, emptiness, and worthlessness made her look into Christianity for the first time in her life with more significance.

FACILITATOR: Role it and action!

PAULA: Mom, why does it bother you so much that I'm not married?

MAMA: Well, honey, when I was growing up, women got married and took care of their families. That's just what they did back in the olden days.

PAULA: But you know things have changed, Mom. Women can do anything they want to today. Some women work outside the home *and* take care of a family.

MAMA: That's true. I guess I'm old-fashioned, but I believe that the good Lord intended for women to be home, looking after things that involve the home. That includes a husband, young'uns, neighbors, schools, and the community.

PAULA: Here we go again.

MAMA: I know, I know. You and your father believe that you will be the first woman president, and neither of you wants to hear an ignorant old woman talk about the old days and what a woman was expected to be.

PAULA: No. I don't want to hear my own mother say in one breath that she's proud of me for all my business accomplishments and then in the same breath say she really feels sorry for me because I'm not barefoot and pregnant.

MAMA: Paula, I've never said those particular words, but I won't lie to you either. I am very proud of all your accomplishments, but sweetheart, at what cost have you done these things? As your mother, I can see that deep down inside you're not really happy.

PAULA:	What you really mean is deep down inside *you're* not really happy for me, because at my age, you expected me to have a husband, two kids, and a big house.
MAMA:	Yes, there was a time when I used to think those were the most important things in life. Now all I want is for you to come to know the Lord. I really believe that it is your next level of fulfillment. I have been very fulfilled as a wife and a mother, but I am more fulfilled as a child.
PAULA:	A *child*?
MAMA:	Yes, as a child; a child of God. I recently came to know Jesus as my Savior, and I want you to know that it has been the most fulfilling decision I've ever made. It has cleared up the feelings of worthlessness I had growing up.
PAULA:	Mom, you had feelings of worthlessness too?
MAMA:	Oh, Lord, yes, but knowing Jesus has changed all that. You see, my mother often made me feel as if I could not do anything right. I know I've said and done things in the past that must have hurt you the same way your grandmother hurt me. I was trying to make you into someone I wanted you to be instead of who you are. I may have been even a little jealous of the things you've done. I was wrong. Will you forgive me, Paula?
PAULA:	Jealous? Oh, Mom, you have never asked my forgiveness for anything, but yes I will forgive you.
MAMA:	Thank you, sweetheart. Now, I need to ask a favor of you.
PAULA:	What is it, Mom?
MAMA:	Will you consider what I've told you about Jesus today?

What do we say? How do you think Paula will respond to her mother's request? Why do you think Paula would be willing to hear more about

Jesus? Can forgiveness bridge a gap in relationships? Have you ever asked someone for their forgiveness? Did he or she give it? Discuss.

What does the *Word* say? Read scriptures from: Matthew 11:28; John 3:16–17, 16:33; Romans 5:8, 10:8–11; Psalms 15–16, 16:11, 34:8, 42:5–6, 86:11–13, 96:1–3; Proverbs 1:7; Ephesians 2:8–10, 4:32; Colossians 3:12–14; James 4:4, 5:1–3; 1 John 2:15–17, 4:18; and Revelation 22:17.

Determine which scriptures apply to each person involved in this case. Can you think of any scriptures to add? In the notes section below, write down your preferred scripture regarding this situation. Memorize it.

Notes

_____

_____

_____

_____

_____

_____

_____

_____

_____

_____

_____

_____

_____

_____

_____

_____

_____

_____

Session 24

Harold, Bianca, and the Bite of the Dragon

Harold was in love with Bianca. He loved everything about her. She was a Christian, pure, clean, and untouched. She was innocent. More importantly, she belonged to him; she was his alone. She made him feel like a man. He loved her so much that he constantly had to know her whereabouts. He wanted her with him as soon as humanly possible. The problem was Bianca had been misled by her family, especially her father. He had caused their break up. Harold knew Bianca's father wanted her for himself. Harold hated her father like he hated his own. He needed to get Bianca away from her father before he defiled her the way his own father had defiled him. He would protect her once he got her away from her father and other men.

He could still hear her voice in his head telling him she couldn't see him anymore because he wasn't a Christian. She told him she couldn't deal with his possessiveness and jealousy any longer. She said he didn't want her to have friends. She said he had deliberately alienated her family and was disrespectful to her father.

Didn't she realize that her father was manipulating her to turn away from him? He acknowledged that he was a little jealous of her male friends, but he couldn't help it. The thought of her with another man made him physically ill. Didn't she understand that *he* loved her? He tried to explain how he felt when he saw her playfully flirting with other guys, but she said that he was imagining things. She accused him of being overly sensitive and suspicious.

Bianca was so naïve. She didn't understand the ways of the world. She didn't realize that his suspicions of these other men were well-grounded, especially after she started her new job. The new job caused her to travel away from home, and sometimes she worked nights and weekends. After she invited him to go to the company picnic as her date and he had gotten into an argument with one of her supervisors for making a pass at her, she'd broken up with him the following day. They had argued. Didn't she understand that he would never let her go? He had become so enraged that he grabbed her and shook her hard. He couldn't remember what happened after that. He must have blacked out. All he remembered was waking up parked under a bridge. He had a few scratches on his face and arms and a bruise by his left eye. He didn't know how he'd acquired them. He hated not being able to remember. It wasn't the first time he'd experienced blackouts, but this time he *had* to remember what had happened.

In desperation, he'd called Bianca so many times he'd lost count. He needed to speak her. He had to let her know he was sorry and he would never hurt her again. He went to her house, but she wasn't there. He went to her parents' house, but they refused to talk to him. He called her best friend, Felicia, hoping to get some answers from her.

FACILITATOR:	Role it and action!
HAROLD:	Hello, Felicia, this is Harold. Uh, have you seen Bianca?
FELICIA:	Oh, hello Harold. No, I haven't seen or talked to her today, why?
HAROLD:	I've called her home phone and her cell, but she won't pick up. She won't answer my texts. I'm going nuts! I *really* need to talk to her.
FELICIA:	Yeah, I can hear it in your voice. Uh, by the way, how did you get my number?
HAROLD:	I have all of Bianca's friend's numbers.
FELICIA:	Wow, seriously?
HAROLD:	Look, I'm not kidding, Felicia, have you talked to her? If you have, would you just tell me the truth?

FELICIA:	I'm not kidding either. The last time I talked to Bianca was yesterday afternoon. What's the matter with you?
HAROLD:	I'm worried about her. I have this feeling that things aren't right. Did she say she was planning to go anywhere special for her job? Did she say anything at all?
FELICIA:	No, she didn't. Look, Harold, you're *scaring* me.
HAROLD:	I'm sorry, but the truth is Bianca and I had a little disagreement. I blew up and said some things I'm pretty ashamed of so I called her to apologize. I went by her house but she didn't answer the door. I can't understand why her car is still in the driveway if she's not there. I need to let her know how much I love her. I *can't* be without her in my life. I *need* to find her. Can you help me out? Would you go over to her house with me, please?

What do we say? What should Felicia say to Harold? Should she go to Bianca's house with him? What is her next step? Why do you think Bianca didn't answer Harold? What does Harold mean when he says he *can't* be without Bianca? What are some dangers of dating a nonbeliever? How should a single person handle an overly possessive friend or even a stalker?

What does the *Word* say? Read scriptures from: Matthew 10:16, 18:7–8; 2 Corinthians 6:14–15,17–18; James 3:14–16; Proverbs 3:31–33, 14:16–17, 16:2, 25, 27:4; Psalms 37:8–9, 38–40, 38:12, 55:3–4, 59:1–4, 73:7, 138:7; Isaiah 55:7; Jeremiah 17:9; Ephesians 6:12–13; and 1 John 1:9.

Determine which scriptures apply to each person involved in this case. Can you think of any scriptures to add? In the notes section below, write down your preferred scripture regarding this situation. Memorize it.

Notes

_____

_____

_____

_____

Annette Richardson

_____

_____

_____

_____

_____

_____

_____

_____

_____

_____

_____

_____

_____

_____

Session 25

Rachel's Gift

Rachel took the day off from work and celebrated her fifty-seventh birthday at home with a Jan Karon audible book a friend gave her for a birthday gift. While she was at home, she prayed for some of her coworkers and then later visited a number of elderly church members who were in the nursing home. She lived alone and found great joy in being able to come and go as she pleased. She loved being able to pray without constantly tending to the needs of a husband and children. Both her parents were dead and she was an only child, but she was content with the life God had given her.

When Rachel returned to work the following week, she was bombarded with questions from her coworkers about how she spent her birthday. When she told them, she saw the pitying looks they exchanged with one another when they thought she wasn't looking. She sighed. They felt sorry for her, and it made her tired.

Later that day, her team leader, Martha, brought pictures of her new grandbaby over for Rachel to admire. After the tenth picture of the little darling, Rachel grew bored and stifled a yawn that nearly escaped her. Mistaking her boredom for longing Martha patted her on the shoulder sympathetically. She reassured Rachel that marriage could still happen for her. If not, had she considered adoption? Rachel sighed again and wished that her coworkers would stop feeling sorry for her because she didn't have a husband, children, or grandchildren to fawn and fuss over.

The Thanksgiving holiday was coming up next Thursday, and she received the perfunctory invitations to dinner from her well-meaning friends, coworkers, and church members, but she graciously declined. She wanted to simply enjoy the holiday by reading and visiting some of her more elderly friends. She could sense her coworkers and church members collectively shaking their heads in sorrow at the poor, lonely, fifty-seven-year-old spinster. Rachel sighed once more and hoped that they all would collectively knock it off!

FACILITATOR:	Role it and action!
AVA:	Rachel, I've been your best friend now for twelve years, and in twelve years you've only spent Thanksgiving with my family once or twice. Why do you keep rejecting my invitation year after year?
RACHEL:	I appreciate your invitations, Ava, but I just want to stay home and relax during the holidays.
AVA:	I can't believe that you would rather be home alone than sharing Thanksgiving dinner with people who love you. It's unnatural, Rachel.
RACHEL:	What's unnatural about it?
AVA:	Honey, even the Bible says it's not good for man to be alone. That means *woman* too. You need to get married. You need a man.
RACHEL:	I'm well aware of what the Bible says, and I'm also aware of the fact that marriage is not the cure for loneliness. When I want company, I go see people. I talk to my friends, I visit the sick. I'm just fine and dandy with the way things are.
AVA:	You're joking about this, but I know it hurts. It hurts for you to see your friends and coworkers with husbands and children and even grandchildren and you don't have anyone of your own—not even a boyfriend. I know you're not gay, but I have to tell you that people have asked me if that's what's wrong with you. Of course I defended you, but it made me ache to find the right man for you to prove to people that you're normal.
RACHEL:	Uh, thank you.

AVA:	You're welcome, but I know you're being sarcastic. Listen, I know that it's just your foolish pride that won't let you admit your pain for what you don't have.
RACHEL:	I have Jesus.
AVA:	I'm serious, Rachel! You're not bad-looking, and you're a good person. You would make some man a very loving wife. You're still young enough. I mean fifty-something is not that old, right? Fifty is the new forty.
RACHEL:	Ava, why don't you believe that I'm content with my life? Why won't you trust the fact that singleness is God's gift to me and I willingly accept it?
AVA:	Because no woman in her right mind believes that. Look, Rachel, John has a cousin who is recently widowed. I think you two would be a good match. I'll talk to John this evening.

What do we say? Is Rachel in denial? Is she too proud to admit that she's lonely and wants a husband? Is singleness a gift from God, or is Ava right in saying that singleness is unnatural? Do people in general tend to pity singles? Do married people sometimes seem smug? Can a person really be single and content? Discuss.

What does the *Word* say? Read scriptures from: Psalm 113:9; Isaiah 54:1, 56:4–5; Matthew 19:12; Mark 12:25; Romans 14:7, 10, 12; 1 Corinthians 2:15, 7:8, 26–28, 32–35; Philippians 4:10–13; 1 Thessalonians 4:11; 1 Peter 4:16; and 2 Thessalonians 3:11–14.

Determine which scriptures apply to each person involved in this case. Can you think of any scriptures to add? In the notes section below, write down your preferred scripture regarding this situation. Memorize it.

Notes:

_____

_____

_____

_____

_____

_____

Annette Richardson

_____

_____

_____

_____

_____

_____

_____

_____

_____

_____

_____

_____

Session 26

Fred, the Carnal Christian

Fred was a self-professed Christian, but he didn't consider himself to be the Bible-thumping kind. As a matter of fact, he hardly read the Bible, but he believed in God. He didn't run around trying to get people to accept Jesus Christ as their Savior. In fact, few people on his job even knew he was a Christian. His motto was, if anybody wanted to know what he believed, they could always ask him. Fred believed that people had the right to live the way they chose and he didn't have the right to cramp anybody's style. He went to church every Sunday. He was on the usher board and as long as God knew his heart that was all that really mattered.

As a child, he grew up in his neighborhood church. He had attended Sunday school, sung in the boys' choir, and been a junior usher. When he graduated high school, he landed a civil service job and married his high school sweetheart, Shirley. They had two children together and later on divorced. After his divorce, Shirley moved away with the kids, but he still talked to them every night.

He got along well with kids, especially his own. However, he did *not* get along with his ex-wife. In fact, there were times when he hated her. She was always on his back, nagging him. She said that he cursed too much, he drank too much liquor, he smoked too much weed, he shouldn't play the lottery, and so on and so forth. She low-rated his friends by saying they were deadbeats and adulterers. She always judged him. She never knew his heart, and he never bothered to explain anything to her. He wasn't the kind to sit around and mope about his divorce. He stayed active. He still retained his membership at the gym and at his neighborhood church. He coached a little league soccer team and helped tutor kids in mathematics in the church's after-school program. On a typical day he would work, volunteer, hit the gym, and then hit the streets. He had never apologized for loving the night life.

For the past two nights, he'd come home and gone straight to bed. When he'd gone to sleep, he had experienced a recurring dream. At the beginning of the dream, he was walking with his ex and two of his friends, Carlos and Ronnie, who were deceased. They were all going down a long, dark corridor in a huge place that felt familiar to him. When they got to the end of the corridor, his ex-wife, Shirley, turned to the right and asked him to come with her. He shook his head no. She went on and then opened a door to a room. She smiled and waved to him, beckoning him to come with her. Just as he started to go with her, his friends grabbed him and pulled him down a long corridor on the left. As they came to a door, it sounded like one big party was going on behind the closed door. People were laughing, talking, and shouting, and he could hear a rushing sound like music. He put his hand on the doorknob. It felt extremely hot. What initially sounded like laughing and shouting now sounded like shrieks of terror and torment.

He woke up each time bathed in sweat and with his heart pumping wildly. He played the events in the dream over again in his mind. It left him feeling vaguely depressed, not knowing what to make of it. He planned to share his dream with his sister that evening over dinner. She always invited him to Sunday dinner, and he'd get her feedback on the dream.

FACILITATOR:	Role it and action!
FRED:	What is this you're handing me to eat, Sis? Everything is all mixed together, and I can't tell what I'm about to eat.
SIS:	The message of my food is the message of your dream.
FRED:	Say what? I don't get the message, but I'll eat it anyway. So, what do you make of the dream I told you about? It's crazy, right? I wake up exhausted. All I want to do is sleep, but I'm afraid I'll dream again.
SIS:	Well, I'm no psychiatrist, but I think you need to straighten up your life.

FRED:	What do you mean? My life is straight. I believe in God. I go to church. I have a good job. I'm active in my community, and I take care of my kids. What else is there to life?
SIS:	What about your relationship with God? How are you living before Him?
FRED:	I just told you.
SIS:	It's not that simple, Freddie. Your spiritual life is all mixed up like the food on your plate.
FRED:	You're talking in riddles just like Shirley does sometimes. You've been talking to her, haven't you? I hate that woman! I know that's where all this stuff is coming from.
SIS:	You shouldn't hate anybody, Freddie, least of all Shirley. I haven't talked to her lately, but I think *God* is trying to talk to *you*. I think He's warning you through your dreams, and I think you'd better pay attention before it's too late.
FRED:	Really? This is a little creepy, Sis. What do you think He's saying?
SIS:	It's obvious to me, but I think you need to pray and ask God for clarity. Read His Word, and stop living like a hypocrite.
FRED:	Me? I'm not a hypocrite!
SIS:	You are if you say you believe in God and live like the devil. Whatever is behind that door in your dream, Freddie, you don't want any part of it, and maybe Carlos and Ronnie represent that part of your life that's going to lead to your death.
FRED:	You're freaking me out, and you're also judging me. I'm a good person.
SIS:	Freddie, I love you, and I'm not judging you. I'm judging your behavior. You do some good things for people, but good works alone won't get you into heaven. Only Jesus can do that. You've got to make a choice. You can't keep straddling the fence between right and wrong.

FRED:	Just because I drink a few beers with my friends and chase a few girls on the weekends doesn't make me the devil, Sis.
SIS:	It doesn't make you a saint either, Fred. Besides, it's more than that. Tell me this: Why don't people know you're a Christian? Why do you hide it? What's different in your life since you say you've accepted Christ?

What do we say? Did Sis and Shirley judge Freddie unfairly? Is Freddie right? Since God knows his heart, does nothing else matter? Name some things Shirley accused Freddie of doing. Are these things associated with Christian behavior? Why or why not? Why do you suppose Freddie never shares his faith or tells anyone he's a Christian? What is a hypocrite? Do you think the Spirit of God warns us about our lifestyles before it's too late? Can a people be saved and still live any way they please? Is it true that once you're saved, you're always saved? Discuss.

What does the *Word* say? Read scriptures from: Isaiah 64:6; Matthew 13: 38–43; Luke 6:46; 1 Corinthians 2:14, 6:18–20; 2 Corinthians 5:17; Romans 3:23, 12: 9–10, 13:13–14; Galatians 5:16–17, 19–22; Hebrews 10:26–29; James 1:22–25, 2:19, 3:13-15, 5:19–20; 1 Peter 1:15–17; and 1 John 1:9–10, 3:9–10.

Determine which scriptures apply to each person involved in this case. Can you think of any scriptures to add? In the notes section below, write down your preferred scripture regarding this situation. Memorize it.

Notes:

_____

_____

_____

_____

_____

_____

_____

_____

_____

_____

_____

_____

Eddie and Keisha— Promises and Pity

Here is a bonus case. This is a challenge for your group to come up with dialogue and scriptures to support the bonus session. In the notes section below, write down your preferred scripture regarding the situation. Memorize it. God be with you!

Eddie and Keisha were high school sweethearts. Eddie was popular, handsome, and the star quarterback on the high school football team. Keisha was shy, quiet, and not very pretty but was devoted to Eddie. She knew he could have his pick of any girl at the school, but he chose to be with her. She dreamed of marrying Eddie someday and having his children. She loved him and would do anything for him.

Eddie liked Keisha. He liked the way she looked up to him and listened to every word he said. He liked it when she baked him cakes and remembered special things about him, like his birthday. He liked it when she came to his house and cooked dinner for him and his mother. Keisha's mother died when she was fourteen. Her father was alive and worked in construction but was rarely at home. Keisha didn't really have anyone to look after her; that's why she needed Eddie.

He always tried to look after her, and when she dropped out of school to have their baby, he promised he would marry her. On the day the baby was born, Eddie swore that as soon as he found a good job, they would get married.

When Eddie graduated, Keisha's father helped Eddie land a job in construction. Most of the construction jobs were out of town, but the money was too good to turn down. Before he left, he promised that he and Keisha would marry as soon as he saved up enough money to buy a house.

While Eddie was gone, Keisha was able to get a small efficiency apartment through government assistance and make ends meet with the money Eddie sent to her. On his last visit, Eddie promised that as soon as he could find stable work in their hometown, they would marry. He then asked her if she would start to look in on his mother for him since she had been under the weather. Keisha could not refuse him but dreaded the idea of having to visit Eddie's mother alone. She never visited her when Eddie wasn't there. For some reason, his mother disliked Keisha immensely but pretended otherwise when Eddie was in town.

One Friday afternoon, Keisha took the baby over to see Eddie's mother. The woman's hostility was so blatant that Keisha asked her outright why she hated her so much. The older woman promptly told Keisha that she was a fool. She told her to wake up. She'd already wasted two years of her life waiting for Eddie. She said Keisha needed to go to church, go to school, and then get a job. Did Keisha want to end up like her? She then told Keisha not to come back to her house until she had done all three things. Keisha was dumbfounded and felt as though she'd been struck across the face.

She lamented all day Saturday over what Eddie's mother had said to her. Was she a fool? Did Eddie really love her or did he only feel sorry for her? The following morning Keisha and the baby went to the old country church near the school. She listened attentively to the preacher. Sunday after Sunday, Keisha felt herself getting stronger spiritually. People were kind to her at the church. For the first time in her life, she really felt alive. She began to believe that she had a purpose in life and that God would help her find it. She mustered up her courage and enrolled in a GED program to get her diploma.

Eddie came home the following month, and after dinner, Keisha told him all that was in her heart. She told him that she didn't want to live the way they had been living anymore until they were married. She said that she'd heard a sermon that made her feel bad about fornicating and not being his wife. She didn't want any more empty promises, and there would not be any more sex until they were *actually* married. She said the Lord wasn't pleased. She also told him she was going to finish her education and she was thinking of becoming a nurse.

Eddie was first stunned and then furious. He didn't know what had happened to her in his absence. He wanted to know who had been putting ideas in her head. He contended that all preachers and church folk were crooked and nothing less than a bunch of hypocrites. He gave her plenty of examples of televangelists and local preachers who had been caught with their pants down. Didn't she know anything? Keisha agreed with him but said she still needed to do what she felt the Lord was leading her to do.

Angry, Eddie told her that her tactics to try to force him to marry her weren't going to work. They wouldn't marry until he was good and ready. He reminded her that she still had their baby to take care of and he wasn't going to pay for daycare. He told her she'd better think twice about what she was about to do. If she became too highfalutin, she just might lose him.

Notes

_____